BRITAIN
IN OLD PHOTOGRAPHS

GREENWICH & WOOLWICH AT WORK

MARY MILLS

Sutton Publishing Limited
Phoenix Mill · Thrupp · Stroud
Gloucestershire · GL5 2BU

First published 2002

Copyright © Mary Mills, 2002

British Library Cataloguing in Publication Data
A catalogue record for this book is available from the
British Library.

ISBN 0-7509-3000-4

Typeset in 10.5/13.5 Photina.
Typesetting and origination by
Sutton Publishing Limited.
Printed and bound in England by
J.H. Haynes & Co. Ltd, Sparkford.

A crowd gathers in Blackwall Lane, 1920s. Black sticky stuff is running in rivers down the road and lying in pools round their feet. One of the giant tanks of molasses at the Molassine works had ruptured and the sticky liquid ran into tramlines with dire results. Molassine made pet food near the entrance to the Blackheath Tunnel and brands such as Vins and Stims were well known. Molassine was also known for the dreadful smell that pervaded the entire area. (*Simon Bass*)

CONTENTS

From the mid-nineteenth century to the mid-twentieth there were several large factories in the area producing specialist, which frequently meant large, items. This is a large dished and flanged head for a pressure vessel made at the Woolwich Road, Charlton, works of G.A. Harvey in the 1960s. It has just come from a press which can be seen in the background – a piece of equipment from the American Birdsboro Company which specialises in large hydraulic presses. *(Steelcase plc)*

INTRODUCTION

It often comes as a surprise to outsiders to learn that Greenwich was once a centre of heavy industry. Most people see it as just a nice place to visit – the Royal Hospital, the National Maritime Museum, the *Cutty Sark* – but it was once a great manufacturing centre with shipbuilding, glass-making and engineering just three of the industries crammed into this part of London.

The area now covered by the London Borough of Greenwich includes a number of what were once separate towns and villages in the county of Kent. Greenwich was a small fishing port at the junction of the Thames and Ravensbourne, and included Deptford across the creek. Further down river was the town of Woolwich and between the two was Charlton; to the south are Blackheath, Kidbrooke and eventually Eltham.

The most notable feature of Greenwich itself is the grand buildings of the Royal Hospital; for many years this was the Royal Naval College and it is now home to the University of Greenwich. This was the site of a Tudor royal palace and when Henry VIII decided to construct a navy, it was natural for the king to establish two dockyards nearby – one at Deptford and one at Woolwich. These two very large workplaces were set up long before the Industrial Revolution and around them grew up many service industries and a tradition of skills. Other military manufacturing establishments were also opened: armaments production and research were concentrated in Woolwich at what became known as the Royal Arsenal. This establishment grew and grew.

Both Greenwich and Woolwich border the Thames and the river was crucial for transport. During the seventeenth and eighteenth centuries riverside industry spread down from the City of London. These were days of great discovery and colonial expansion, and ships were needed as adventurers, and the investors who followed them, went out to exploit the world's resources. It was on the riverside below London that most of their vessels were built and to which the ships returned laden with goods. Great complexes of docks were built in the surrounding areas during the nineteenth century and as sail turned to steam, Greenwich, Woolwich and Charlton became home to an engineering industry that used skills learned in the dockyards and at the Arsenal.

Greenwich and Woolwich were also centres of innovation and research. The Arsenal itself, birthplace of both the Royal Artillery and the Royal Engineers, included the Royal Military Academy which, together with the Greenwich Observatory, brought many scientists to the area in the eighteenth century. In the decades that followed new initiatives got under way all the time. For instance, in 1836 the first railway to enter London came to Greenwich – and the brick arches on which it ran were built by a military engineer who learned his skills in Woolwich and then on the battlefields of the Peninsula War. Trains have daily pounded over those brick arches ever since.

Another innovation made Greenwich the 'home of communication'. The earliest telegraph cables were made here in the nineteenth century and world production was concentrated in the area for a long time. Today the technology necessary to expand the internet is being pushed along by Greenwich industries.

The list of all the now commonplace items that were developed in this part of London is much too long to give here but an account of some of them appears in the pages that follow, together with some of the people who were involved at every level of their creation. These were people proud of the things they helped to make – the steam engines, the warships, the big guns, the cables, the largest gasholders in the world, the first electrical generating station, the motorcycles and much, much more. Along with manufacturing came the service industries – shops, doctors, schools and everything that we take for granted.

By the 1970s few ships still came up river to the docks, coal was no longer used in the gas works and power stations, and so decisions were taken which meant an industrial heartland and skills built up over 500 years were no longer needed. Along the road from Greenwich through Charlton to Woolwich factories were closed. It all happened very fast and many thousands of people lost their jobs. In the late 1980s you could sit beside the deserted river – more empty than it had been for 1,000 years – and feel that the end of the world really had come at last.

This book ends with some pictures that are about a hope for the future. Greenwich has had to look again not only at the complex of royal buildings but at what else we have that can be sold to the world. All those brown-field sites are being turned over to new uses, hopefully ones that will continue the traditions of skill and innovation from which Greenwich and Woolwich have made a living for so long.

An apparently rural view of Greenwich Marsh in the early nineteenth century. This drawing shows marshland and barns on the Greenwich Peninsula and a view of the distant town. In the background are the domes of what was then the Royal Hospital. However, the picture is much more industrial than it appears. The trees and foliage are osier beds – willow grown commercially for basket making. Although there were many farms in the area now covered by Greenwich and Woolwich, fields on the Peninsula had been leased commercially since at least the late seventeenth century. *(London Borough of Greenwich)*

1

High-Tech Industry in the Nineteenth Century

Mr Blakely, Mr Bessemer and some other gentlemen inspecting progress at their new gun foundry at Blackwall Point, *c.* 1865. The foundry was financed with money from the international opium trade: it was intended to make guns to rival those of Woolwich Arsenal and to sell them abroad. Henry Bessemer, who developed the Bessemer converter for steel manufacture, had become interested in Blakely's manufacturing process and worked with him. Sadly for Blakely, shortly after this picture was taken the money ran out. He was soon to die in mysterious circumstances in Peru. The Millennium Dome now covers most of this site but the name Ordnance Wharf lives on in the area. Nearby cottages were built for the foundry workers and although these have long gone, a café for lorry drivers still has the address Blakely Cottages.

(London Borough of Southwark)

This road vehicle – a car with a steam engine – was built in the 1840s by Frank Hills. He was an industrial chemist with works in Deptford and on the Greenwich Peninsula, and this car was just a sideline for him. A number of steam-driven vehicles were built in Greenwich but there were practical problems with the design and the idea never succeeded. When the cars were new they were usually driven up Shooters Hill in order to attract publicity. They stopped at The Bull near the top of the hill for refreshment – after all, steam cars often needed to take on more water. In this picture Frank Hills is shown urging his driver forward. *(Mechanics Magazine, 1840s)*

John Penn's marine engine factory stood in Blackheath Road and had an entrance from Cold Bath Lane (now John Penn Street). The first John Penn had come from Bristol to open the factory in 1799 and built his first marine steam engine in 1825. Under his son the factory became world famous. At this works the engines were made for many important and ground-breaking ships. New types of engine to propel the biggest battleships were developed here, one well-known example being the engines for *Warrior*, which was built on the Thames and is now berthed as a tourist attraction in Portsmouth. Other important projects were undertaken by Penn's, including the development of the first ever wind tunnel and in due course steam-driven cars and lorries. The factory, which had employed 800 highly skilled workmen, closed in 1911. This picture was taken in about 1860. *(From P. Barry, Dockyard Economy, 1863)*

The interior of the works of the National Company for Boat Building by Machinery on the Greenwich Peninsula, *c.* 1863. The blurred figures are operating the latest high-tech steam-driven machinery. The photographer was P. Barry and his shadow can be seen in the foreground. The National Company was started by an American, Nathan Thompson, who planned to make 4,000 identical small boats each year using a highly mechanised production line system. This was so efficient that he produced far more than he could sell and went bankrupt after the first year. *(From P. Barry, Dockyard Economy, 1863)*

This jetty was built on the tip of Greenwich Peninsula for Blakely's new armaments factory in about 1865. The works is only half built (note the pile of bricks) but one of Blakely's new guns is already loaded on a carriage. Blakely's process for the manufacture of guns had been rejected by the British government and he therefore planned to sell abroad. Orders had already been secured from Russia and America, most notably for the Confederate battleship *Alabama*. On the other side of the Thames is the white bulk of the Brunswick Hotel and the masts and chimneys of riverside industry. *(London Borough of Southwark)*

This dramatically lit drawing shows metal-working at the Royal Arsenal. Work at the Arsenal was widely illustrated in the Victorian period when its achievements were appreciated. Here molten metal is being poured into moulds, probably for shells. The Arsenal was a tremendous resource for many other factories in the Greenwich and Woolwich areas, providing ready trained, highly skilled workers as well as a strong technological research base. *(Jack Vaughan collection)*

A 'Woolwich Infant' so called 'by way of a joke on its size' – or because of the bulge around the breech area. These weapons must certainly have given a mighty roar! Woolwich was very proud of its 'infants' and a local pub is named after them. Other pubs had images of them in tiled wall pictures, one of which is now in the Clockhouse Community Centre. The name seems to have applied to fifteen specific guns with a 12-inch bore and weighing 38 tons, but the authorities differ on whether they were smooth-barrelled or rifled. Perhaps there were examples of both. *(Jack Vaughan collection)*

2

The Ubiquitous River

Greenwich and Woolwich have the longest stretch of riverbank of any London borough. Until very recently the noise and bustle of river work dominated local life. The river provided a means of transport for many goods and services and a glance at a nineteenth-century map will show how industry was positioned to use the river rather than the road system. This ship is at the wharf of Woolwich power station in the 1950s. She is probably a collier bringing coal from north-east England and the cranes are unloading her. The coal was used in the power station to generate electricity. In the distance is one of the 'old' twin-funnelled Woolwich ferries, the 'free ferry' of which Woolwich was so proud. The power station was demolished in the early 1980s and a new public park and riverside walkway now cover much of the site.

(London Borough of Greenwich)

The sailing barge *Pretoria* airing her sails at Ballast Quay, 19 September 1954. The Cutty Sark pub had only recently been renamed – older Greenwich residents still call it the Union Tavern – and this view will be instantly recognisable to anyone using the Greenwich riverside walk today. Barge builders and operators had used Ballast Quay for centuries but by 1954 *Pretoria* was no longer at work and when this picture was taken she was being converted into a floating home. Behind her is a forest of riverside cranes, now all gone. This area is expected to be developed for housing during 2002. *(Patricia O'Driscoll)*

The river seems to be at the end of every street . . . and here it is glimpsed down Bell Water Gate, Woolwich, in the 1950s. On the north bank there are ships – perhaps even a liner – in the King George V Extension to the Royal Group of Docks. When this picture was taken it was unthinkable that 'The Royals' would ever close. 'Water gates' like this allow access to the river and can be found all along the bank. Many of them are protected by ancient rights and statutes but most are now derelict and unused, although in the 1990s one licensed waterman began a campaign to get them restored. Bell Water Gate still exists in theory but a massive new leisure centre now covers most of the area shown in the photograph – and the big ships in the docks are long gone. *(London Borough of Greenwich)*

The Siemens factory on the Woolwich/Charlton border was founded in 1863 and had a distinguished record in the manufacture of telecommunications equipment. In 1956 it was acquired by AEI and the picture shows representatives of the new owners standing on part of the roof area. They were looking for a place to put a new sign to advertise the company's name to river traffic. At this date shipping was regarded as so important that such a sign would mainly be visible to passing river traffic, not to that on the roads. Beyond is the Victoria Dock, itself crammed with cranes and shipping. Slightly left of centre is the Tate & Lyle factory – the only institution in the picture still at work today. *(London Borough of Greenwich)*

A new roof being constructed at Deptford power station in order to cover an extension of the works used to supply power to the Southern Railway, *c.* 1925. Men are working high up above the town using a 'Scotch derrick'. The river is nearby but can hardly be seen in the murky Deptford fog. Across the roofs of terraced housing is a gasholder and there are some other industrial buildings in the distance. Visibility was never very good near the river in the days of coal-fired power. Historically Deptford was part of Greenwich and this site is still in Greenwich Borough. The power station site itself has recently been covered with new housing. *(London Borough of Greenwich)*

Looking down river towards Greenwich from near Deptford power station. A freighter is moored in the river off Greenwich. The view looks over the roofs of wharves on the banks of the Thames and Deptford Creek. In the middle distance are the domes of the Royal Hospital and beyond that smoke from the chimneys of London County Council's Greenwich power station is blowing towards the camera. None of these buildings is really very far away from the camera but the smoke-filled gloom apparently exaggerates the distance. *(London Borough of Greenwich)*

This pre-1940 advertisement for the Greenwich Inlaid Linoleum Works includes a drawing of the linoleum factory on the Greenwich Peninsula with its riverside wharves. Linoleum was invented by Frederick Walton and in the 1890s he came to Greenwich to build a factory that could put into practice his third development in the manufacturing process – the production of patterned linoleum. Three enormous machines were installed at the site which is now known as Victoria Deep Water Wharf. Greenwich linoleum was sold all over the world and river transport was crucial not only for moving the finished product, but also for bringing in raw materials. The picture illustrates very well the importance of the river as distinct from the road transport network. *(Forbo Nairn)*

The Siemens' cable ship *Faraday 1*, 1880s. Specially built and designed by William Siemens himself in 1874, she had two separate engines and two screws to make her more manoeuvrable when laying cable. There were also special parallel twin funnels to make more room for cable storage. She was a regular presence in the river off Woolwich and laid many important underwater cables all round the world. Many other cable ships were also based on the Thames including *Ocean Layer*, *Mercury*, *Colonia* and *Telconia*. *(John Ford and Siemens Engineering Society)*

Tower Shipping's coaster *Tower Julie* delivering 850 tons of maize to the Amylum Factory, which was then still known as Tunnel Glucose, 1960s. She is a rather larger vessel than this photograph indicates, being just under 500 tons, and is still at work, although she is no longer seen on the Thames. Maize was used to manufacture glucose at Amylum until the mid-1990s when complaints about the smell persuaded the company to switch to a wheat-based process. This wheat is delivered by lorry via the Blackwall Tunnel. The silos and the wharf are still on the riverside but are unused. Behind them is the now demolished No. 2 gasholder of the East Greenwich Gas Works. *(Patricia O'Driscoll)*

The amount of smoke around this ship produced by her two attendant tugs completely obscures the vessel's name. The picture dates from soon after the Second World War and was allegedly taken in order to show the need for smoke control. *(Patricia O'Driscoll)*

The Transfenica ship *Maria Borthon* heading down river past Canary Wharf, 1990s. She is a 'ro-ro' – 'roll-on, roll-off' – vessel and has just delivered paper for newsprint to Convoys Wharf on the site of the old Royal Dockyard, Deptford. *Maria Borthon* is now empty and riding high in the water; despite her size she is fast and surprisingly manoeuvrable. Except for the occasional cruise liner or visiting warship, these were the last big ships to be seen above Woolwich. Convoys was the wharf furthest up river to remain in commercial use late into the twentieth century but it closed in 2000. The old Royal Dockyard will soon be redeveloped for housing or something similar. *(Howard Chard)*

Bringing Coal to London

Greenwich and Woolwich factories depended on coal-fired power, and the coal mainly came by sea and river from the pits of north-east England – Durham and Northumberland. This is the jetty at East Greenwich Gas Works on the Greenwich Peninsula, which was built in the early 1880s and is shown here in the 1920s. The jetty handled 1¼ million tons of coal a year which came by collier ship from the north-east. The 4-ton cranes were all hydraulic – no electricity allowed in the gas works! On the lower part of the decks were workshops and mess-rooms for the staff who ran the jetty as an establishment separate from the rest of the works. Today a small section of the jetty remains and is part of the pier built to serve the Millennium Dome. It is the site of an artwork by Anthony Gormley called *Quantam Cloud* – and by a strange coincidence Gormley's *Angel of the North* now stands beside the A1 and dominates the old Durham coalfield. *(A Century of Gas Lighting)*

The Harbour Master's House, Ballast Quay, *c.* 1970. This house was built in the mid-1840s as a residence for officials attempting to control the vast numbers of collier ships in the Thames. The ships were moored at collier stands in the river awaiting their turn to discharge their cargo at special wharves. The house stands on the corner of Pelton Road, named from Pelton Main colliery in County Durham, and the road behind it was once called Newcastle Street. It is now a private residence and has appeared in many films. Film-making is one of the growth industries in this area today. (*London Borough of Greenwich*)

The coaster *Cornelia Bosna* discharging her cargo at Lovell's Wharf near the Harbour Master's House which can be seen at the far right-hand side. Lovell's Wharf is next to Ballast Quay and was originally built in the 1840s for the coal trade by a Mr Coles Child. He leased a large area on the edge of the Greenwich Peninsula, which was previously fields, and built riverside wharves. At the same time he provided several streets of terraced housing for workers and these streets were named after Durham pit villages. Although in this instance the cargo being handled is metal bars, the scene is nevertheless reminiscent of the days when north-eastern coal would have been taken ashore here. (*By kind permission of Shaw Lovell. Photograph Derek Rowe*)

By the middle of the Victorian period so much coal was coming into London by ship that special measures had to be taken to deal with it. In the 1850s William Cory conceived the idea of building a system out in the river for unloading the coal and transferring it into barges. This involved mooring a hulk called *Atlas* in the river and fitting it out with cranes. The whole noisy, dirty structure was sited in Bugsby's Reach off the east bank of the Greenwich Peninsula. By 1875 1½ million tons of sea coal were being unloaded here every year. The top picture shows *Atlas 1*, which remained in use until 1910, and below is *Atlas 3*, which was specially built and installed in 1898 and then removed for war work in 1915. Although in both pictures the jumble of cranes and funnels is sometimes difficult to interpret, basically there is a central hulk with a superstructure and around it are moored steam colliers together with some lighters. The name 'Atlas and Derrick Gardens' in Anchor and Hope Lane, Charlton is a reminder of this system and was originally built to house Cory's workers. *(above, Cory Environmental; below, London Borough of Greenwich)*

The South Metropolitan Gas Company's brand new collier ship, *Dulwich*, in the Thames off East Greenwich. While a great deal has been said about the lives of coal miners and the gas works stokers, rather less is known of the hard lives and heroism of sailors who brought the coal to London down the treacherous east coast. *Dulwich* was only to be in service for fourteen months. In June 1916 she was torpedoed off Lowestoft. The lifeboat could not be lowered. Nevertheless, all but three of the crew were pulled from the sea. The engineer and fireman had already died in the engine room. *(from Co-partnership Journal)*

Another South Metropolitan Gas Company collier, this time the *Ravensbourne*, lying new off East Greenwich in 1915. She had a life of less than two years. On 21 January 1917 an hour after leaving the Tyne with a cargo of 1,950 tons of coal she was struck. Captain Macfarlane thought the vessel had been torpedoed. She went down in about three minutes. One lifeboat was launched and fifteen of the crew were saved although the chief engineer, H. Harrower, the Second Engineer, T. Gilfoyle, and the 'donkeyman', W. Carter, went down with the ship. Captain Macfarlane survived a total of three torpedo attacks. South Met was to lose its whole fleet of colliers twice over during the First World War, yet their crews were sometimes taunted by the public who saw the men as cowards who had refused to join the army. *(from Co-partnership Journal)*

The constant river traffic needed constant maintenance. Bargeyards and boatyards were part of a whole network of businesses that serviced the river trades and included lighterage and tug companies, mast- and sail-makers. Here Jim Farey and Alf Blackman are finishing off repairs on the big motor barge *Olive May* at Piper's Yard in East Greenwich in the 1960s. Some new wood is being let in to her stem following damage in the docks and Alf is using an adze to do this. This is a cutting tool with an arched blade set at right angles to the handle and is relatively unusual. Pat O'Driscoll, the photographer, had waited a long time for an opportunity to take a picture of the tool in use. Barge repair work was highly skilled and men had to serve apprenticeships. In Greenwich barge builders had their own trade union which later became part of the Transport & General Workers. *(Patricia O'Driscoll)*

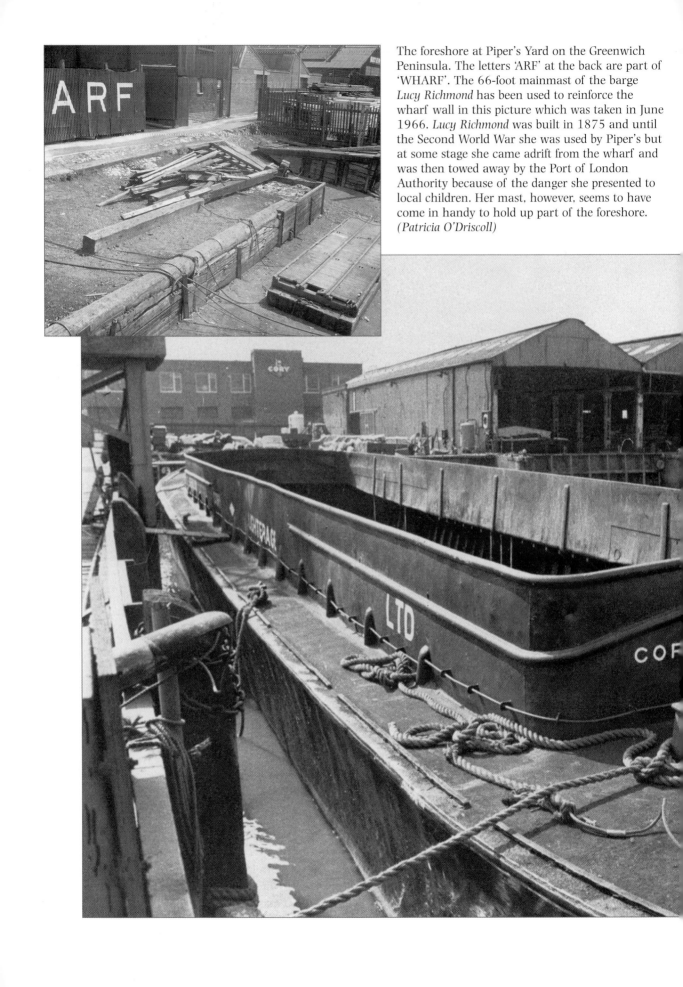

The foreshore at Piper's Yard on the Greenwich Peninsula. The letters 'ARF' at the back are part of 'WHARF'. The 66-foot mainmast of the barge *Lucy Richmond* has been used to reinforce the wharf wall in this picture which was taken in June 1966. *Lucy Richmond* was built in 1875 and until the Second World War she was used by Piper's but at some stage she came adrift from the wharf and was then towed away by the Port of London Authority because of the danger she presented to local children. Her mast, however, seems to have come in handy to hold up part of the foreshore. *(Patricia O'Driscoll)*

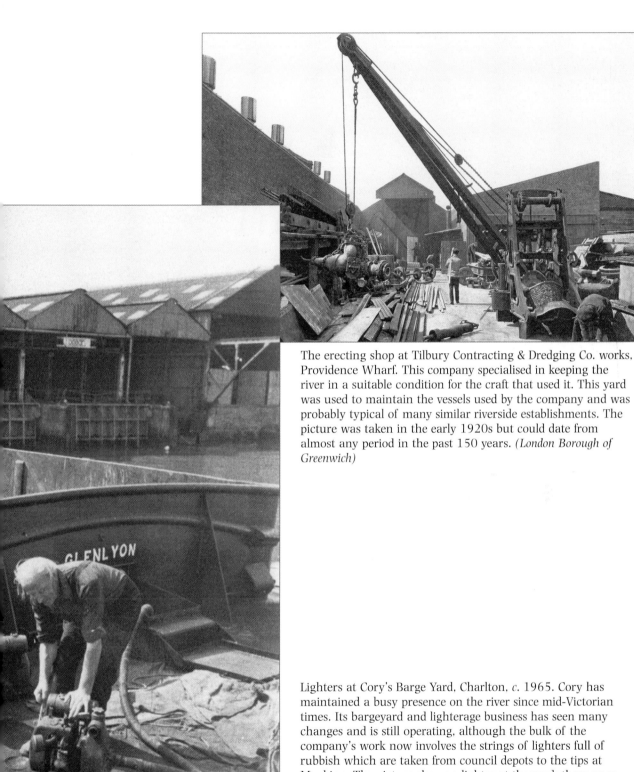

The erecting shop at Tilbury Contracting & Dredging Co. works, Providence Wharf. This company specialised in keeping the river in a suitable condition for the craft that used it. This yard was used to maintain the vessels used by the company and was probably typical of many similar riverside establishments. The picture was taken in the early 1920s but could date from almost any period in the past 150 years. *(London Borough of Greenwich)*

Lighters at Cory's Barge Yard, Charlton, *c.* 1965. Cory has maintained a busy presence on the river since mid-Victorian times. Its bargeyard and lighterage business has seen many changes and is still operating, although the bulk of the company's work now involves the strings of lighters full of rubbish which are taken from council depots to the tips at Mucking. The picture shows a lighter at the yard; these once-common craft are seen much less frequently today. They are large open vessels without engines and their way of working has evolved over centuries. Until the 1980s there were many lighterage firms along the riverside employing lightermen who had served an apprenticeship and were registered to work as such. *(Cory Environmental)*

Sailing barges were the workhorses of London's river and many famous race winners were built in Greenwich. There were many barge businesses – building and repairing barges, lighters and other small craft. Norton's on the east bank of the Greenwich Peninsula survived into the 1950s but by then it was a repair business only.

These barges were photographed at Norton's Yard, Bugsby's Hole, at Easter 1957. Working outwards they are *Clara*, *Adriatic*, *Oxygen* and *Beatrice Maud*. All were still at work. *Oxygen* and *Beatrice Maud* were at Norton's because work was slack and this berth saved them having to lie on the Woolwich buoys which their skippers disliked. *Adriatic* was in the early stages of being converted into a motor barge. *Clara* was eventually sold 'up river' to be used by a scout troop and the others still exist as hulks. These 'spritsail' barges had evolved as a style specially adapted for the Thames and were both practical and cheap to run. Their good looks mean many have survived, taken on by enthusiasts once they were no longer needed as working vessels. *(Patricia O'Driscoll)*

Norton's bargeyard, seen from the river, 1957. In fact, photographer Pat O'Driscoll took this picture from the rigging of the barge *Oxygen*. Beyond the riverside path are the sheds and cranes of Redpath Brown's structural steel works, later British Steel. In the foreground are all the bits and pieces that make a working barge repair yard – wood, cable, some trestles. Parallel to the shore are a number of barge blocks on to which craft were floated at high water and then secured. When the tide ebbed men could work on the underside of the vessel. A great deal of detritus and the remains of some blocks remained on the foreshore after Norton's closed but all this was cleared in 1999 as part of the rebuilding of the riverside for the Millennium Experience. *(Patricia O'Driscoll)*

Dick Norton with Fred Bayley, the watchman, at Norton's Yard, 1961. Norton's had two sheds; one was for storing tools, nuts, bolts, etc. and the other was Fred's living quarters. Fred was Norton's last employee and the facilities he used were through a wicket gate in the corrugated iron fence of the Dorman Long factory where there was a tap for water and a heap of coal. The water was used for a steam crane which was also on the site. *(Patricia O'Driscoll)*

Sailing barge *Ardwina* being repaired at Norton's, 1955. *Ardwina* is still active and in sail, albeit for leisure use. She was built in Ipswich in 1909 and converted a few years after this picture was taken. A 66-ton barge, she is made of wood. *(Patricia O'Driscoll)*

Skipper Harold Smy working on the sailing barge *Beatrice Maud*, which he had commanded for thirty-eight years. The picture was taken in 1957 when work was slack. Harold had put in to Norton's and taken the opportunity to paint the barge's decks with the usual blue/grey mixture – but being careful to do only half the deck at a time. *(Patricia O'Driscoll)*

The sailing barge *Verona* at Pear Tree Wharf, 16 March 1955. *Verona* was actually a Greenwich barge, having been built in 1905 by Horace Shrubsall at the tip of the Peninsula. Her days 'in trade' were already over when this picture was taken; her fate and her current location are not clear, although it is thought she may be in Stockholm in use as an artists' studio. Norton's Yard was not far from where she was built, and in the distance are various riverside factories including the chimneys of Stone's Anchor Works and the tanks of Esso's site at the end of the Dorman Long works. All of this area is now landscaped as a park and Pear Tree Wharf is now the site of Greenwich Yacht Club's super new clubhouse and marina. *(Patricia O'Driscoll)*

In the 1980s and 1990s the transfer of aggregates became a major feature of the remaining industry on the Greenwich riverside. Here aggregate is being transferred into a lighter from a works at Angerstein Wharf, the only railhead left on the river. The single tower of Canary Wharf, on the other side of the river, is in the background. In front of them on the Greenwich Peninsula are the few remaining buildings of Blackwall Point power station, with the Port of London Authority's radar scanner on top. These were some of the last buildings to be demolished before the Millennium Experience opened. *(Howard Chard)*

This picture and the one below show Lovell's Wharf on the Greenwich Riverside in the 1980s. Lovell's Wharf is on the edge of the western bank of the Peninsula adjacent to Ballast Quay. Originally built in the 1840s as a coal wharf, it was used by Shaw Lovell from the early 1920s, mainly for the transhipment of metals. Lovell's maintained a part of the London Metal Exchange here and in the 1960s built an office block as its head office. This block still stands and is used by Greenwich Council; just inside the door is a huge doormat with 'Lovells' written on it. The Scotch Derrick cranes are transferring metal rods from a coaster which lies alongside the wharf and the Harbour Master's House on Ballast Quay can be seen in the background. *(By kind permission of Shaw Lovell. Photograph Derek Rowe)*

It was never easy for large ships to access Lovell's Wharf. In the 1980s Shaw Lovell attempted to refurbish the wharf and a large amount of money was spent on the two remaining cranes. Trade did not come back to the wharf, however, and it remained derelict and empty, except when it was used by the ubiquitous film companies, always in search of a location. The two cranes were demolished in 2001 in the face of local protests from those who saw them as the last vestiges of traditional river work. *(By kind permission of Shaw Lovell. Photograph Derek Rowe)*

Part of the coaster *Luminence* at Piper's Wharf on the Greenwich Peninsula, 1970s. *Luminence*, built in 1954, was owned by the London & Rochester Trading Co. To the right of the picture is the cable ship *John W. MacKay* which was moored at Enderby's Wharf for many years. She was built in 1922 and equipped with cable-laying machinery designed for her by the Telegraph Construction & Maintenance Company, to which she belonged. She was refitted in 1965 but remained at the jetty until she was sold. For many years cable layers like her were a constant feature of this part of the river. In front of her are a number of lighters, one loaded with a cable drum and another with aggregate. *(Howard Chard)*

The Charlton riverside was the last resting place of many ships and barges. Here, in the 1950s, a wooden sailing barge has been hauled up on to the foreshore at Garratt's Barge Breakers, perhaps to be broken up. The most famous ship breaker was Castle's, also at Charlton. It is said that Castle's works was distinguished by an enormous pile of timbers taken from old ships, many of which would have been built in Deptford or in Woolwich dockyards. *(Patricia O'Driscoll)*

3
Gas & Power for Heat & Light

East Greenwich had one of the most remarkable gas works ever built – the South Metropolitan Gas Company's plant. It was built in the 1880s – which is very late for a gas works – and combined the very latest technology with the very highest standards. In the 1880s under its charismatic Chairman, George Livesey, the company introduced a profit sharing – 'co-partnership' – scheme with idealistic principles. This Christmas card to employees gives some idea of what the scheme was about: the left-hand panel shows work in the gas works' retort houses and the right 'a life of ease' in retirement thanks to hard work and savings. The centre panel shows Charles Elbourn's 'Temperance Cottage'; it is likely this was a now-demolished house in Annandale Road, East Greenwich. *(from Co-partnership Journal)*

The Greenwich Peninsula – now the site of the Millennium Dome – in the early 1920s when the South Metropolitan Gas Company's works was at its height. The works was built in the early 1880s and included a huge complex of chemical facilities and associated plant. There have been claims that it was the biggest in the world and certainly the gas company's aspirations for this works were enormous. The two huge gasholders – No. 2, the shorter, was the biggest in the world – symbolised a commitment to the very latest technology and the very highest standards of public service. The river snakes around the Peninsula past ships, jetties and docks in a busy world of industry and work. Coal brought by sea from north-east England was the raw material from which the gas was made. At the end of the nineteenth century gas lit and often powered factories as well as homes, while gas tar and other waste products fed the surrounding chemical industry. *(A Century of Gas)*

The old sulphate house at East Greenwich Gas Works. Many chemical by-products were an essential part of the gas-making process. About twenty years after its foundation the South Met acquired a chemical plant, which it called Phoenix, on the south side of the site. Phoenix produced sulphate of ammonia which was sometimes sold as a fertiliser and this giant building was used to store it. In 1956 it was demolished and replaced by an amazing pre-cast concrete structure which remained there into the 1990s and was much used for pop videos by the ubiquitous film companies. (*from Co-partnership Journal*)

A gas-powered ambulance. It is the First World War, fuel is short – and so the gas company decides that its product can be used to propel vehicles. This is the South Metropolitan Gas Works Air Raid Rescue Party with all their equipment and their ambulance. The gas is stored in an enormous balloon on the roof. Near the front of the vehicle hangs a diving suit – essential for rescue workers who might have to go into a gas-filled chamber. South Met was understandably a very safety-conscious company and any accident had to be investigated by a panel of workers chosen at random. (*from Co-partnership Journal*)

Women gas workers at the South Metropolitan Gas Works during the First World War. It is not entirely clear at which works these pictures were taken, since they are probably posed by models, but they almost certainly show the great East Greenwich works. Women workers were taken on from 1915 – and promptly got rid of in 1919 when the men returned. The top picture shows women in the retort house which demanded hard, hot and heavy work, normally only undertaken by the very strongest men. The woman shown is replacing the cover of the furnace below the retorts. Flame comes from the retorts from which coke has been removed. Below, women are filling and lifting hundred-weight sacks of coke. Coke was sold to industries and homes locally – and in peacetime it was thought that women could only manage sacks of half this weight. (*Brian Sturt*)

The two gasholders at the South Metropolitan Gas Company's East Greenwich works, *c.* 1900. The picture is taken from Blackwall Lane; today this is the A102M Blackwall Tunnel Approach Road. These two holders combined represent the largest capacity of gas storage ever and were built to revolutionary engineering principles. The holder nearest the camera, No. 1, is still in use but it stands alone; its companion was demolished in 1986. As the photograph shows, shops, houses and St Michael's Church once stood nearby but today everything except the pub and No. 1 holder has gone. *(London Borough of Greenwich)*

Inside No. 2 gasholder, the largest ever built in Britain and for many years the largest in the world. On 19 January 1917 east London was devastated by an explosion in a Silvertown munitions works across the river. In the gas works 'the floor appeared to heave, the building rocked, followed by a blinding glare' – the blast had ruptured the gasholder and 12 million cubic feet of gas burned safely high in the air above Greenwich. The picture shows the clean-up operation and the tiny figures of the workers with their wheelbarrows are dwarfed by the enormous structure. *(from Co-partnership Journal)*

Demolition of No. 2 gasholder, 1986. This picture was taken across the snowy wastes of what had been East Greenwich Gas Works. No. 1 gasholder stands still full of gas. In the distance are the cranes for container transshipment at the Victoria Deep Water Terminal. The area is now covered by the outbuildings for the Millennium Dome and No. 1 holder stands alone on the approach road. *(Mary Mills)*

A sailing barge lies alongside at the wharf for Woolwich power station and a crane is being used to load – or unload – bales. It is not entirely clear what the bales contain – or even whether they are anything to do with the power station. A man stands looking down at the barge and another appears to be controlling the crane to the right. On the buildings behind is a painted advertisement for the Northern Coal Company based in Charlton and Woolwich. Generating stations were built alongside the Thames throughout the twentieth century and used the same basic raw material, coal from the north-east. *(London Borough of Greenwich)*

LCC's electricity generating station at Greenwich was constructed to provide power for London's trams. The jetty appears to be finished but the two rear chimneys still stand alone. This power station survives on the Greenwich riverside and generates electricity for London Underground, but the collier ships no longer call at the jetty. There is now a large, and unused, coal bunker on the right-hand side of the station. Then, as now, the tiny buildings of the Trinity Almshouses are dwarfed by the power station. *(London Borough of Greenwich)*

A lone power station worker stands at the control panel of a small power station. This is one of two photographs donated to the London Borough of Greenwich Local History Library with a note to say that it was believed they dated from 1909 and showed the interior of the London County Council generating station at Greenwich (above). Expert opinion does not think that this is the LCC station but it may be somewhere else in Greenwich. Anyone who recognises this picture is encouraged to contact the author. *(London Borough of Greenwich)*

The world's first power station in the modern sense was built in Deptford in 1889. This original was designed by a young man called Sebastian de Ferranti. Electricity was generated here and then sent a hitherto unheard of distance at 10,000 volts AC to supply light to central London. The picture shows the original Ferranti generator. In due course Ferranti's works was superseded by Deptford West and Deptford East power stations. Operations finally ceased in 1983. The site is now covered with flats and houses – and there is no mention at all of the first power station in the world. *(London Borough of Greenwich)*

White Hart Road Depot was built by Woolwich Borough Council in 1903 as a power station where electricity could be generated from the Borough's waste. This revolutionary building still stands in White Hart Road, Plumstead. Dustcarts would trundle up the long ramp in front of the building and tip their rubbish in the hall beyond. From there it would be fed into furnaces to provide fuel for the generation of electricity used for street lighting in the area. Electricity generation stopped in the 1920s but the building continued as the Borough depot until 2001. It is now used as a film studio. *(London Borough of Greenwich)*

A woman worker manages two chain-grate boilers standing side by side at Johnson & Phillips cable works in Victoria Way during the Second World War. Claude Johnson and Samuel Phillips opened a works in Victoria Way, Charlton, in 1875 for the manufacture of telegraph cables and their company became one of the major cable makers in the area. Although the worker might be adjusting the flow of fuel at the mechanical stokers at the front of the boiler it is more likely that she is standing there to create a good picture! *(Delta plc)*

The boilerman examines the gauge glasses of the boilers at the Royal Arsenal Co-operative Society's Commonwealth Buildings site in the late 1950s. These boilers provided all the heat and power for RACS and what was in effect a factory complex providing services for the whole of the Co-operative Society's network of shops. It was a centralised boiler system and hot water was transferred around the site through overhead pipes. One very visible relic of Commonwealth Buildings is the huge chimney which stands alongside Woolwich Church Street and which is being renovated as a feature of the old dockyard area in a regeneration scheme. *(RACS Archive)*

4

Transport

The Woolwich Free Ferry was opened in 1889 by London County Council to great rejoicing
and celebrations locally. The idea was to give east London a free river crossing because tolls
had already been abolished on bridges in the centre and west of the city. Here the ferry boat
Gordon is in mid-river on her way between Woolwich and North Woolwich. The picture
shows the original *Gordon* built in 1888; it was later replaced by another vessel of the same
name. In 1963 she too was replaced by the current ferries which still provide a regular
service. Until 1966 the area north of the river was in Kent, and thus part of Woolwich
proper. To this day those who live there refer to Woolwich town as 'South Woolwich'.
(London Borough of Greenwich)

Future torpedo boat manufacturer Alfred Yarrow in his experimental steam-driven car, 1861. Yarrow was only twenty years old and together with two friends he had commissioned this steam car from Mr Cowan at the Kent Iron Works by Deptford Creek. This vehicle was driven to Bromley (with the inevitable stops at local pubs 'because the engine needed water') and the story goes that an old lady who saw the noisy, smoky party late at night thought they were the Devil. Thirty years later steam lorries were to be made at the old Penn factory by Thames Ironworks. (*London Borough of Greenwich*)

A cart for house-to-house deliveries of a temperance beverage. Such deliveries persisted into the 1950s but this smart pair and their drivers are owned by Willson's Horehound Brewery based in Eastney Street, Greenwich and the picture dates from 1906. Horehound beer is a herbal drink: note the advertisement on the cart for sarsaparilla, ginger ale, ginger beer and 'Kola'. In the background is a semaphore signal for the South Eastern Railway which means the picture was probably taken on the railway bridge in Maze Hill where a signal post is today the cause of local annoyance since train drivers sound their horn there. (*London Borough of Greenwich*)

The men sitting on the South Metropolitan Gas Company's new car are a breakdown crew going to repair an escape of gas in 1910. When South Met decided to phase out its horses the men who managed them were retrained as motor mechanics. Vehicles were purchased to a company standard as far as possible and used to get to emergencies. Gas leaks clearly required prompt action and with a speed of 20mph these vehicles were four times as fast as 'Dobbin'. Of course, the motor spirit on which these cars ran was all manufactured in the company's tar depot at Ordnance Wharf. *(from Co-partnership Journal)*

Delivery vans at W.F. Stanley's instrument works at New Eltham in the 1950s. The original Mr Stanley had been a major force at South Norwood where there are several monuments to him, including a clock tower, a technical school and a community hall. The company eventually moved to New Eltham, only closing in 2001. Here packing cases holding the delicate precision equipment manufactured by the company are loaded into Stanley's own fleet of vans. *(from Stanley Company History)*

Delivery lorries at the loading bay of the Delta Metal Factory on the west bank of the Greenwich Peninsula, 1960s. 'Delta Metal' is a bronze alloy developed locally at the end of the nineteenth century and the Delta Metal factory was opened on the Greenwich Peninsula in 1905. Some sheds still stand on the site. The company remained in Greenwich until the 1980s but by then production had moved to the Johnson & Phillips factory in Victoria Way, Charlton. During the Second World War the company claimed that Delta's brasses and bronzes could be found in almost every item 'from the largest battleships to the smallest launches . . . tanks to lorries'. *(Delta plc)*

This wartime picture shows a young woman driving a small Lister truck at the Johnson & Phillips factory in Charlton. Johnson & Phillips were cable-makers with a large factory which was eventually taken over by Delta. The truck holds one of the massive reels on which cable was loaded for transport. The older, uniformed woman is described as the 'gate-keeper' and both are part of a drive to recruit women to undertake factory work during the Second World War. *(Delta plc)*

The London & Greenwich Railway was the first suburban line in the world, and the first steam railway in London. The principle of 'Sail before Steam' meant that the rail bridge across Deptford Creek had to be capable of opening. Here in 1963 a Southern Electric train is crossing the creek on the 1884 version of a bridge first constructed in 1838 while a lighter rests on the mud below – perhaps it has been rowed in traditional fashion with the single oar resting against the side. This narrow gap had to be negotiated by all Ravensbourne traffic going up river to mills and works above the railway line. It is said that a dozen or so men were needed to open the bridge if a taller vessel needed to go through. *(John Ford and Siemens Engineering Society)*

In 1964 the current lifting railway bridge was built across Deptford Creek. In order to complete cable links across it a special 'Night Excursion' train was laid on for engineers from the AEI (Siemens) Cables Division. The lighterman has pulled himself clear of the mud and is now floating in on the incoming water. The lifting bridge is still in place today although it is apparently never used since ships no longer go right up the creek. *(John Ford and Siemens Engineering Society)*

'The Angerstein Line' was built in 1852 by local landowner William Angerstein entirely on private land and ran from a junction near Charlton station down to a riverside wharf. This view is remarkable in that it shows a railway line and a road; both still exist but a six-lane motorway was built between them in the 1960s. *(London Borough of Greenwich)*

A goods trains heads down towards Angerstein Wharf, 2000. It has come through the tunnel which runs under Blackheath and behind it can be seen the buildings of the old Southern Railway signal works, now a trading estate. The train is probably loaded with stone destined for the large aggregate processing plant at Angerstein Wharf. At one time this line served a whole network of rails on the Greenwich Peninsula and in Charlton. One branch headed into East Greenwich Gas Works and another to the United Glass Factory in Charlton, both serving other factories en route. Today neither the Sainsbury's warehouse which replaced the glass factory nor the operators of Millennium Dome need to use the railway, but loads of stone are still carried to the riverside. *(Howard Chard)*

Walter Hancock's steam coach *Era* advertising a journey between London and Greenwich. The picture dates from 1832 when Hancock was running such services in central London. Steam road buses appeared slightly earlier than the first suburban railways and were designed to provide regular passenger services by road. It is not known what form this Greenwich service took or how often it ran but it is unlikely to have been able to compete with the Greenwich Railway, built in 1836. *(from Mechanics Magazine)*

A Sentinel steam wagon belonging to the South London Motor Transport Company. The wagon is shown alongside Gioachino Veneziani's Charlton factory, which made an 'anti-fouling compound' – an anti-corrosive paint for ships. Veneziani's opened here in 1903 at the request of the British Admiralty. The manager at the time was the famous Italian author Italo Suevo and a plaque can be found on his home in nearby Charlton Church Lane. Veneziani's factory closed in 1913. *(Veneziani (Italy))*

The Merryweather fire engine factory in Greenwich High Road. A fire engine stands at the entrance and seems to be causing some excitement. Is it a new machine undergoing trials? Merryweather's fire equipment was famous and the company was good at staging stunts for publicity purposes – more usually they involved fire hoses and astonishing jets of water. Among the crowd of onlookers are the usual small boys – and passengers on top of a passing open-top tram en route to Westminster Bridge. Trams had become a feature of Greenwich and Woolwich life around the turn of the century and the London County Council repair depot at Feltram Way in Charlton was itself a busy workplace. (London Borough of Greenwich)

The Tramatorium. London's trams found their last resting place in Charlton. As tram services ended in the early 1950s, the defunct vehicles were brought to a site off the Woolwich Road in Charlton and broken up. The final tram, driven by Alf Jago, Mayor of Woolwich, arrived there in July 1952. There was great public emotion about the end of the trams. 'Last Tram Week' was sponsored by the London County Council. This picture was clearly taken through the wire fence of the 'Tramatorium' by an enthusiast eager to get a last photograph of these popular vehicles. (London Borough of Greenwich)

The Woolwich ferry crew and two policemen whose beat included the ferry, *c.* 1900. In the centre is the captain, 'Skipper' Thomas Terry Tucker. In 1917 'Skipper' married Edith Nesbit, author of *The Railway Children*. He was described by her up-market friends as 'a common little man who never wore a collar'. *(London Borough of Greenwich)*

The 'penny ferry'. This ferry was opened in about 1847 by the Great Eastern Railway Company. It was intended to transfer passengers who had travelled from London Fenchurch Street to North Woolwich on to the South Eastern Railway services to the Kent coast. Here the ferry boat *Kent* is seen on the Woolwich foreshore and there are a number of sailing craft on the river including a spritsail barge in full sail. The 'penny ferry' continued for some years after the opening of the free ferry but closed in 1908. *(London Borough of Greenwich)*

Two sorts of transport at Deptford. In the railway arches are the usual motor repair shops and purveyors of MOT certificates. The railway arches themselves are something more unusual. In 1836 the London & Greenwich Railway became the first in London and the first suburban railway in the world. The project was full of new ideas: the designer of the arches, Lt Col George Landmann, intended that carriages and carts would go up on to them from the road. The idea was that vehicles would be taken from the road up the slope and loaded on to railway wagons on the arched viaduct high above; they could also be used for rolling stock. This is the inclined plane at Deptford, consisting of stepped brick arches around three sides of a square. There is no real evidence that this system was ever used and the structure has remained a home for small workshops – latterly the motor trade – ever since. *(Mary Mills)*

Reclaim the streets! Motor traffic has clogged the streets of Greenwich for nearly a hundred years. The Borough suffers more than most because of the bottleneck effect caused by two lots of river crossing – the Blackwall Tunnel to the north and Deptford Bridge and Creek Bridge to the west. A party of demonstrators closed Romney Road at its junction with Nelson Road in 1996 in protest at traffic levels. *(Mary Mills)*

5

The Royal Arsenal

One of the great steam hammers at the Arsenal.
The original 40-ton hammer was first used in 1874
by no less a person than the Tsar of Russia. The
remains of these huge hammers still lie somewhere
underground at the Arsenal, too big and too heavy
to be removed even by the scrap trade. The base of
one of them – perhaps this one – is likely to be put
on display near its original site as part of the new
Greenwich Heritage Centre. *(Jack Vaughan collection)*

The real industrial strength of Greenwich and Woolwich was in engineering and nowhere was this more strongly demonstrated than at the Royal Arsenal. This was an institution whose size and complexity was simply stunning. The Arsenal grew out of The Warren where storehouses, a ropewalk and various other buildings were joined by the Royal Laboratory in 1695. The Royal Military Academy was founded here, as were both the Royal Engineers and the Royal Artillery. The complex included the Royal Gun Factory and the Royal Carriage Department. By 1907 the Arsenal covered 1,285 acres and stretched for 3 miles down river – at its peak 80,000 people worked there. There was an internal canal system with a lock on to the Thames and 120 miles of standard gauge railway which had its own timetable, as well as a narrow gauge system. The pictures that follow can only give a glimpse of this amazing place.

  This photograph dates from about 1875 and seems to show a large gun being tested in some way – is it perhaps being weighed? The caption on the back of the picture says that it is in a box beam made for mounting 38-ton guns in high casemates and that this was a 12.5-foot long 38-ton rifled muzzle-loaded gun which fired a 818lb shell a little under 6 miles using a 210lb load of propellant. Note the hydraulic jacks which enabled the barrel to be positioned exactly horizontal so that the sight markings could be checked. *(London Borough of Greenwich)*

A long line of blacksmiths' hearths stretching into the distance at Woolwich Arsenal. An ex-Arsenal worker commented, 'I don't remember the forge being this big – but then the one I worked in wasn't the main one!' This picture, like several of the others in this chapter, comes from a series of postcards produced in 1914, perhaps sold to raise money for the war effort. *(Jack Vaughan collection)*

The bullet foundry, *c.* 1914 . This is probably where the business end of the bullet was produced. The photograph shows one of the many vast floor areas of the Arsenal with line shafting (a mechanical means of driving machinery) and a bustle of workers. In the foreground a worker turns to look at the camera; he clearly isn't the foreman since he doesn't have a bowler hat on, so why is he out of his place at the workbench? *(Jack Vaughan collection)*

This picture may show the other side of the shop floor seen in the picture at the bottom of the opposite page. There is the same line of workers at benches down the centre of the building with line shafting above them, and in the foreground is the row of machines. At the height of its work during the First World War the Arsenal contained many, many shop floors like this, turning out weapons to arm the soldiers of the king. *(Jack Vaughan collection)*

A gun jacket is bored at Woolwich Arsenal and a worker peers at the job in hand, *c.* 1914. The distinctive structures above the shop floor identify this as the Arsenal and not one of the other armaments factories of the day. *(Jack Vaughan collection)*

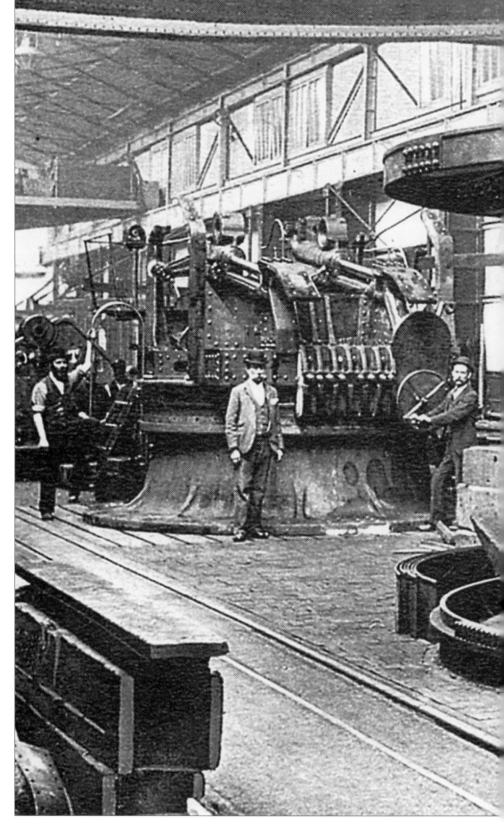

A Moncreiff disappearing gun mounting, *c.* 1907. This is a heavy naval gun mounting although one ex-Arsenal worker said, 'It's not what I would call heavy'! The guns shown are for firing shells for coastal defence. There is a 6-inch weapon in the background and in the foreground a 9-inch. Guns like this were sent around the world to defend the British Empire. This is Building C58 and in the twentieth century it was known as the 'slide shop'. Jack Vaughan's workbench was behind the guns shown. (*Jack Vaughan collection*)

Brass foundry, 1914. This is not in the 1716 listed building now known as 'The Brass Foundry'; at this time that had other uses. *(Jack Vaughan collection)*

This postcard, dating from about 1914, is captioned 'pot fines' and as such is something of a mystery. Clearly some sort of firing is in hand – but what does 'fines' mean, or is it a misprint for 'fires'? The wheeled implements are to remove and transport red hot items to other parts of the building. *(Jack Vaughan collection)*

Cartridges being made, *c.* 1914. The blanks on the left are ready to be set up. The cylinders in the foreground are more of a mystery since they are solid; for cartridge manufacture they should be hollow. *(Jack Vaughan collection)*

A 6-inch gun barrel being bored or 'rifled' . The guns are moved forward on 100hp works motors. This picture also dates from about 1914 and was taken at the South Boring Mill. *(Jack Vaughan collection)*

In the 1990s it was decided that a number of the buildings should be used as a museum and heritage centre. Firepower, the Museum of the Royal Artillery, was the first to open and other buildings (like the one shown in the picture) are to be used by the London Borough of Greenwich. *(Chris Stevens, London Borough of Greenwich)*

Workers in Woolwich Dockyard and the Arsenal realised early the benefits of forming co-operative societies to provide quality goods and services to their members with mutual benefits. The earliest traced society dates back to the 1760s but the Royal Arsenal Co-operative Society (RACS) itself was formed in 1872. The statue of Alexander McLeod, the first Secretary of the Society, stands over the door of the department store in Powis Street, Woolwich. *(London Borough of Greenwich)*

In 1926 RACS built a manufacturing complex at Commonwealth Buildings on part of the old Woolwich Dockyard. This plaque was installed there in the 1930s but was gone by the end of the Second World War. Its exact location is not clear but it was probably alongside today's Co-operative Funeral Buildings in Woolwich Church Street. At its height Commonwealth Buildings employed 1,500 people in twenty-one different trades. The picture shows some of them – Co-op milk, of course, but also vehicle repair and maintenance. At the back left of the picture is the chimney which still stands in Woolwich Church Street. (*RACS Archive*)

The coachbuilders' shop, Commonwealth Buildings, 1929. Clearly it was important to keep the fleet of RACS delivery vehicles on the road, particularly in the days when a much greater proportion of goods was delivered to families who had no access to private transport themselves. Although the wheels which lay all around are clearly from horse-drawn carts there is also a smart van being fitted out with timber work and other vehicles to the rear. Compare this picture with the image on page 41 of the gas fitters' car owned by South Metropolitan Gas Company at a similar date. (*RACS Archive*)

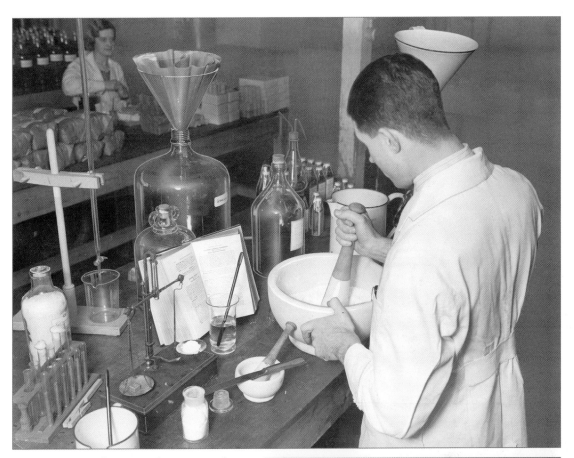

RACS maintained its own pharmacy and laboratory at Commonwealth Buildings. The laboratory was eventually to move to Mitcham. RACS produced its own brands of cosmetics and medicines which were made here. Local people remember pots of cold cream labelled 'Manufactured by RACS, Commonwealth Buildings'. This pharmacist is clearly using a recipe book to make up his mixture with pestle and mortar. The picture was taken in the 1950s. *(RACS Archive)*

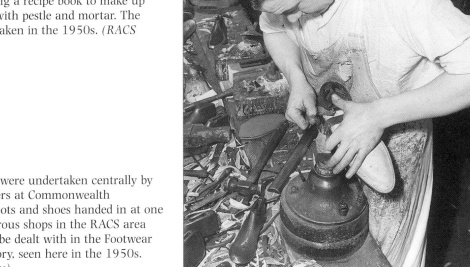

Shoe repairs were undertaken centrally by skilled cobblers at Commonwealth Buildings. Boots and shoes handed in at one of the numerous shops in the RACS area were sent to be dealt with in the Footwear Repairs Factory, seen here in the 1950s. *(RACS Archive)*

RACS maintained a butter packing plant at Commonwealth Buildings. Butter was sent there from all over the world – former workers remember a Polish consignment. There it was blended together into a mix and sold as 'Creamery Butter'. This butter, duly wrapped, was then sent out to one of the many RACS grocery stores in the area. *(RACS Archive)*

Model-maker Bert Fulling working at Commonwealth Buildings on a window display for one of the many RACS shops in Greenwich and Woolwich and the surrounding district, 1960s. This specialist window display department operated until the end of 2001, albeit by then the work was done in Dartford. Although this is a window display Bert's smart commissionaire is holding a menu card, perhaps describing the dishes of the day at the RACS restaurant in Powis Street. *(RACS Archive)*

A wartime view of the Smiths' Shop at Commonwealth Buildings. This was part of the Wheelwrights' Shop and here men are working at forges. All maintenance work for RACS was done at Commonwealth Buildings and many items were made there in-house rather than purchased from outside. *(RACS Archive)*

A worker in the RACS Grocery Warehouse at Commonwealth Building weighs a packet of dried fruit, 1960s. Many dry groceries were delivered and packed for the Society in this way. *(RACS Archive)*

A cutter at work in the Tailoring Department at RACS Commonwealth Buildings establishment, 1960s. The RACS bespoke tailoring department was in Powis Street, Woolwich. There you could be measured for a suit 'same as at Burtons' and the order would go to the Tailoring Department. *(RACS Archive)*

A worker in the dry cleaning department at Commonwealth Buildings operates a steam form for taking the creases out of a newly cleaned coat, 1963. Items needing to be dry cleaned were handed in at one of the numerous RACS retail outlets in the area and brought here to be cleaned centrally by specialist staff. *(RACS Archive)*

The milk bottling plant, 1963. Everyone knows that the Co-op was the only source of milk in the days of groundsmen who went from door-to-door. This is the bottling plant at Commonwealth Buildings which was situated parallel to Woolwich Church Street behind the wall near where the chimney still stands. The bottled milk was then sent to a number of depots around the area and then delivered to doorsteps by milkmen. *(RACS Archive)*

The bacon stoves stood behind the buildings which are now part of the Co-operative Funeral Service. RACS smoked all its own bacon which was then distributed to shops throughout the area. Smoking is an unpleasant trade, but the few who can be persuaded to do the work are often perfectionists. Although RACS operated its own piggery at Woodlands Farm this was not used for bacon but for Christmas 'locally grown and killed' pork. This picture was taken in the 1950s. *(RACS Archive)*

The traditions of the co-operative movement have been inherited from RACS and are still active in Greenwich and Woolwich in the twenty-first century. The group of black cab drivers to which this man belongs functions as a co-operative to provide a mutual telephone booking service. (*Greenwich Co-operative Development Agency*)

This Greenwich-based orchestra brings together top-class performers into a mutual society, which allows them to provide concerts and recitals in local venues. The group is standing in Greenwich Park overlooking the National Maritime Museum. Beyond is the single tower of Canary Wharf. To the right are the four chimneys of the Greenwich (London Underground) power station. (*Greenwich Co-operative Development Agency*)

6

The Home of Communication

For nearly 200 years Greenwich and
Woolwich have been at the forefront of
communications technology. The development
of submarine cables for the early telegraphs
led to the establishment of a number of
factories to make them. These developed and
widened their activities to include many other
devices. Today only the Alcatel site on the
Greenwich Peninsula remains but there
components are still produced which speed
messages through the Greenwich-made cables
that now encircle the whole world. This is no
exaggeration: during the nineteenth century
and much of the twentieth two-thirds of the
world's submarine cable was made at the
Telcon (now Alcatel) works. The remaining
cable manufacturing was undertaken in
factories a short distance away – Siemens at
Woolwich, and Johnson & Phillips at Charlton,
the Gutta Percha Works and Henleys across
the river, and Callenders at Erith.

This worker at Telcon in the 1950s is carefully
examining the core of cables, probably made
using the Telcothene insulation method
developed at Greenwich before the Second
World War. *(Alcatel)*

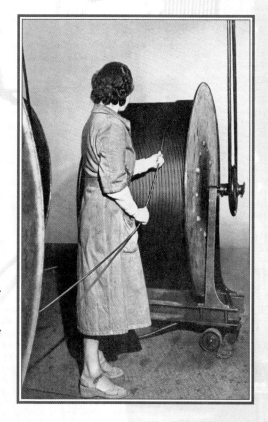

Enderby Brothers' factory burning down at Greenwich, 1845. Enderby Land in the Antarctic is named after this family who made rope and canvas for their fleet of whaling ships here in the early nineteenth century. The wharf has been known as Enderby's ever since. The family's rope-making business moved into cable-making and the works was taken over by specialist cable-makers who developed the business still further. Some of the earliest submarine cable was produced here, including the first Atlantic cable. In this drawing the factory is well alight. The watching crowd is a considerable distance away on the riverbank, somewhere near Ballast Quay. *(London Borough of Greenwich)*

Morden Wharf is slightly down river from the Enderby Brothers' site. In the early 1860s a company called Glass Elliott opened the works shown here and made the cable used in the first attempt to put a telegraph line across the Atlantic. The picture shows Glass Elliott's works with the giant tanks in which the manufactured cable was coiled and stored before being taken out to a ship. The cable had to be in one piece, so the tanks had to hold enough cable to stretch across the Atlantic! Soon after this picture was produced Glass Elliott moved to Enderby's Wharf which was then vacant and the successful Atlantic cable was made there. *(London Borough of Greenwich)*

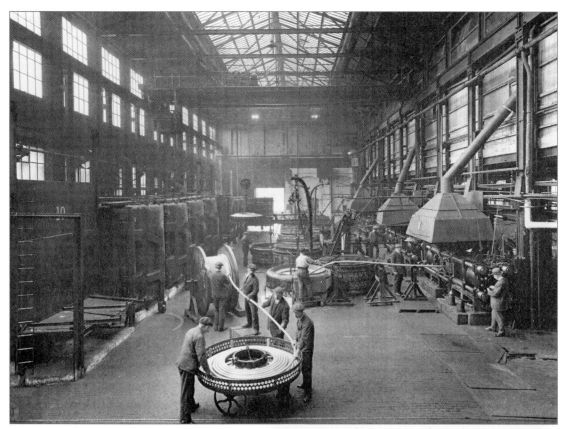

Cable being covered with lead at the Siemens Works, Woolwich, 1920s. This is obviously an extremely dangerous job and needs a high degree of skill as well as caution. The cable is being put into a tank to receive its lead coating. At the same time cable is fed out of the storage trays and on to a reel for transport. *(John Ford and Siemens Engineering Society)*

A worker watches a wire-drawing machine at the Telcon Works on the Greenwich Peninsula, 1950s. The twisted wires will be the basis for the final cable. The first companies who moved into cable manufacture in the nineteenth century had often started off in the manufacture of wire rope. Although the Telcon Works is best known for its submarine cables the company also produced a range of alloys of great importance as technology in electronics developed. *(Alcatel)*

Circular vulcaniser trays being prepared at the Siemens factory, Woolwich, 1940s. Vulcanisation is the process by which rubber is mixed with sulphur and heated to 140°C. This increases the rubber's strength, reduces porosity and removes smell without damaging the material's insulating qualities, thus creating an ideal protective cover for electrical cables. *(John Ford and the Siemens Engineering Society)*

Mechanised lifting of vulcaniser trays at the Johnson & Phillips factory, Charlton. This Second World War picture was taken at a time when much labouring work was being undertaken by women. One of the workers is operating the heavy lifting gear. Women were sometimes seen to be more careful than men and therefore useful in moving difficult loads. *(Delta plc)*

Coiling down cable in a tank, Siemens, 1920s. The cable is fed carefully in and guided by hand into its place. *(John Ford and the Siemens Engineering Society)*

Cable being led across the Greenwich riverside path at Enderby Wharf to a ship on the river, 1950s. The river and the wharf itself are to the left of the picture and the cable is coming from the Telcon factory to the right. On the other side of the fence is Enderby House, an 1840s building used as offices by Telcon. The first successful Atlantic cable was laid from Brunel's great ship the *Great Eastern* – the biggest ship then built, which was launched close by at Millwall. It is said that the mast shown in the centre of the picture came from the *Great Eastern* and was used to hold sensitive instruments above the level of the ship's magnetic field. Although the path has not changed very much, and Enderby House is still there, the cable and the mast are long gone. *(Patricia O'Driscoll)*

The Telcon factory, Greenwich, 1940s. The site, which has provided jobs in high-tech industries for nearly 140 years, is substantially the same today. It stands on the west bank of the Greenwich Peninsula – Blackwall Lane can be seen in the foreground. The long cable sheds cover the line of an early nineteenth-century ropewalk, and by the river stands an 1840s house once occupied by the Enderby family. Today the site is owned by Alcatel which manufactures repeaters for submarine cable; the modern factory is to the left of the older cable sheds. A ship is shown moored at 'dolphins' in the river. Vessels moored here were usually special cable ships, but this seems to be a different sort. Cable was paid out from the factory to ships, and today some preserved equipment remains on the jetty. In the 1950s a small ferry ran between the dolphins and the shore. To the right of the picture a road runs from Blackwall Lane to Greenwich Council's jetty. This was used by dustcarts going to tip rubbish into barges for disposal. *(Alcatel)*

The main office at Siemens' Woolwich factory, 1880s. William Siemens opened his works at Charlton in 1862. It originally consisted of a few single-storey wooden buildings with cable-making machines and an engine. The factory soon expanded to take over neighbouring premises and the first brick building went up in 1865. In the early years rapid expansion of the telegraph network meant that the factory was very busy but the increase in electrical inventions – the telephone, arc lamps, etc. – was to guarantee its future. *(John Ford and the Siemens Engineering Society)*

For many years cable ships were a constant sight in the river. Here cable is being loaded from a lighter on to a ship at Enderby's Wharf during the time when the factory was owned by Telcon. In this instance the cable is wound on to reels. Equipment for transferring continuous cable from the factory on to ships is still preserved at Enderby's Wharf today. *(Alcatel)*

Rows of young women assembling telephones in the Siemens' factory at Woolwich, 1920s. These are 'candlestick' telephones and each worker has a box of parts beside her. Siemens had become involved in the manufacture of telephone equipment shortly before the First World War and special buildings were provided at Woolwich for this branch of its work. Young women were employed by Siemens from 1896 and, as some of the following pictures show, were to make up an important part of the workforce. (*John Ford and the Siemens Engineering Society*)

These men are assembling manual telephone exchanges in the 1920s. Clearly the complex equipment is to be hidden behind some quite smart joinery. At this stage Siemens was already developing new and important arrangements. To some extent this work had been held up by the First World War but by the 1920s, following decisions by the Post Office, Siemens was manufacturing exchanges on a large scale and was also deeply involved in developments using the most advanced technology. It was to make the first automatic exchange and the Woolwich factory was the first in the world to have one fitted. (*John Ford and the Siemens Engineering Society*)

The Neophone was a major step forward both for Siemens and for the telephone service in general. It was developed by Siemens in the late 1920s and the design was formulated in association with the British Post Office. It became one of the most familiar pieces of everyday equipment and was used in various forms for nearly fifty years. It remained a major production item at the Woolwich works. *(John Ford and the Siemens Engineering Society)*

Soldering a joint in the wiring section of the Telecommunications Department at the Woolwich Works, 1960s. AEI had by then taken over the plant from Siemens Brothers. This young woman is doing essentially the same highly skilled work at the Woolwich factory as her grandmother would have done. *(John Ford and the Siemens Engineering Society)*

Egyptian visitors to the Siemens' works test out new telephone systems with one of the company's leading technical staff, 1960s. The telephone they are holding is a later version of the Neophone. *(John Ford and Siemens Engineering Society)*

A military party at the Siemens Works in 1943 embarks on a visit to inspect work on the Pluto wartime fuel pipeline. It is believed that the figure on the far left is Field Marshal Montgomery. Clearly this visit was top secret and it is thought that the picture must have been taken illegally. A new building had been erected at Siemens for work on Pluto and two pipelines were made there – 2 inches in diameter and 35 miles long. Each weighed 2,000 tons. Siemens had already suffered devastating bombing during the Second World War; the first air raid on the Thames on 7 September 1940 targeted the docks north of the river and Siemens in the south 'with cool deliberation and devastating effect'. *(John Ford and Siemens Engineering Society)*

7
Engineering Skills

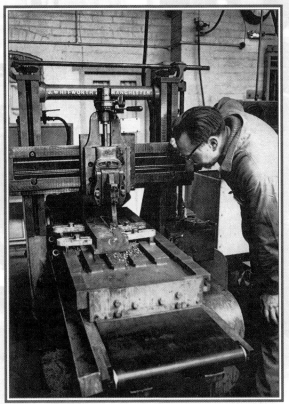

The Whitworth planing machine No. 623 at Eltham.
This antique piece of machinery was photographed
in the 1960s at Walter Grafton's, an engineering
company which occupied a strange crenellated
factory building in Foots Cray Road, now the site of
a superstore. The machine dates from the late
nineteenth century and was probably originally sold
to a tool cutter based in Westcombe Park. Despite its
age it was still accurate to 0.0001 inch over table.
The fate of the machine after Grafton's closed is not
known. (*from London's Industrial Heritage. Photograph
Joseph McKeown*)

J. Stone & Co was founded as an engineering works in the arches under the Greenwich railway at Deptford but the growth in the number of propeller-driven steamships led it to open a foundry in Charlton in 1916. This Charlton propeller works made equipment for some of the most glamorous Atlantic liners. These pictures from the 1930s show the preparations for producing the propeller for the *Queen Mary*. A mould was made for a propeller casting built up of bricks on an iron foundation plate. Top right is a striker board which moves up and down on a central shaft and will eventually give an exact reproduction of the final curved surface. In a vessel like *Queen Mary* the tips of the propeller blade would travel through the water at 60mph, creating constant vortices in the water and subjecting the blade to persistent hammering from all directions. *(J. Stone & Co.)*

One of the 35-ton propellers made for the *Queen Mary*. It has a diameter of nearly 20 feet. The casting weighed 53 tons and the mould in which it was cast weighed over 100 tons. The cast bronze took ten days to cool. The men who made the casting were said to work on it with 'military precision . . . not a word is spoken and every man knows exactly what he has to do'. The Charlton factory also made the propellers for the liners *Queen Elizabeth*, *Normandie* and *Empress of Britain*. *(J. Stone & Co.)*

The planing machine used to make propellers at Charlton – the only one of its type in the world. The cutting tool moves back and forth across the propeller blades at about 80 feet a minute. The propeller must have an extremely fine and accurate finish, and although this machine was extremely advanced the work still had to be finished by hand. Getting the massive propeller from Charlton to the *Queen Mary* presented a problem; it was taken by road to the Surrey Docks and then loaded on to a ship before being taken to the Clyde shipyard to be fitted *(J. Stone & Co.)*

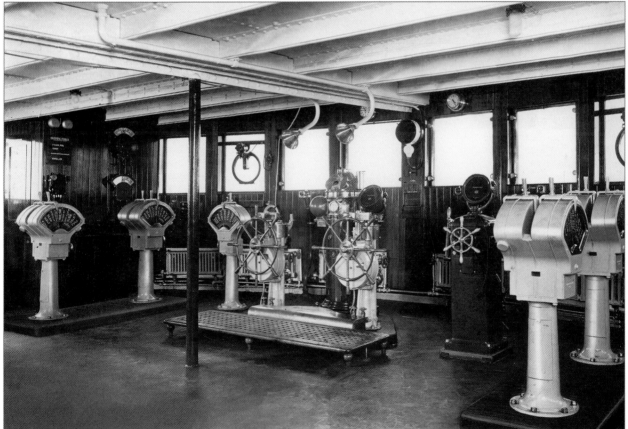

A different part of the *Queen Mary* and a different factory. The instruments on the Cunard liner's bridge were made by Siemens. Although Stone's was in Charlton and Siemens in Woolwich, the factories were in fact very close to each other – Stone's at the bottom of Anchor and Hope Lane and Siemens adjacent to the current site of the Thames Barrier. *(John Ford and Siemens Engineering Society)*

A group of firemen demonstrating their 'Telephone and Air-Helmets', probably in Greenwich High Road, *c.* 1900. These helmets were attached to pipes which carried both a supply of fresh air and telephone wires to keep the men in contact with their supervising officer. The firemen are also carrying electric lamps. The steam fire engine shown is typical of many made by Merryweather's to a range of different designs and exported all over the world. (*Author's collection*)

Merryweather's factory stood in Greenwich High Road and although the company made a wide variety of equipment, fire engines were its speciality. This 1880s drawing shows Fire Pump Enfield. This particular design was worked out specially for the British War Department for use at the Royal Enfield small arms factory, hence its name, but examples were sold to places as far away as Rio de Janiero and Wiborg. Its special design meant the boiler could not explode and the pump could be worked using foul water. (*Ted Barr*)

A 45MVA transmission transformer being prepared at the Johnson & Phillips Works in Victoria Way, Charlton, 1960s. Today the site of this factory is covered with housing. *(Delta plc)*

A 113-foot fractionating tower for the BP Chemical Plant at Baglan Bay in Wales to be used to produce propylene, 1960s. Such towers were made at Harvey's Charlton factory for chemical works all over the world. G.A. Harvey moved to Woolwich Road from Lewisham in 1911. The company originally specialised in galvanised tanks – coating the structure with a zinc surface – but then began to diversify. During the Second World War Harvey's produced vast quantities of metal gauze and all sorts of perforated metal and wirework. By the 1950s they were making metal furniture and office fittings. *(Steelcase plc)*

Opposite below: A 72-ton machine in the Perforation Department at Harvey's, 1960s. The 12-gauge steel plate is being punched with $\frac{3}{16}$-inch diameter holes to a National Coal Board specification. It will be used for screening coke. *(Steelcase plc)*

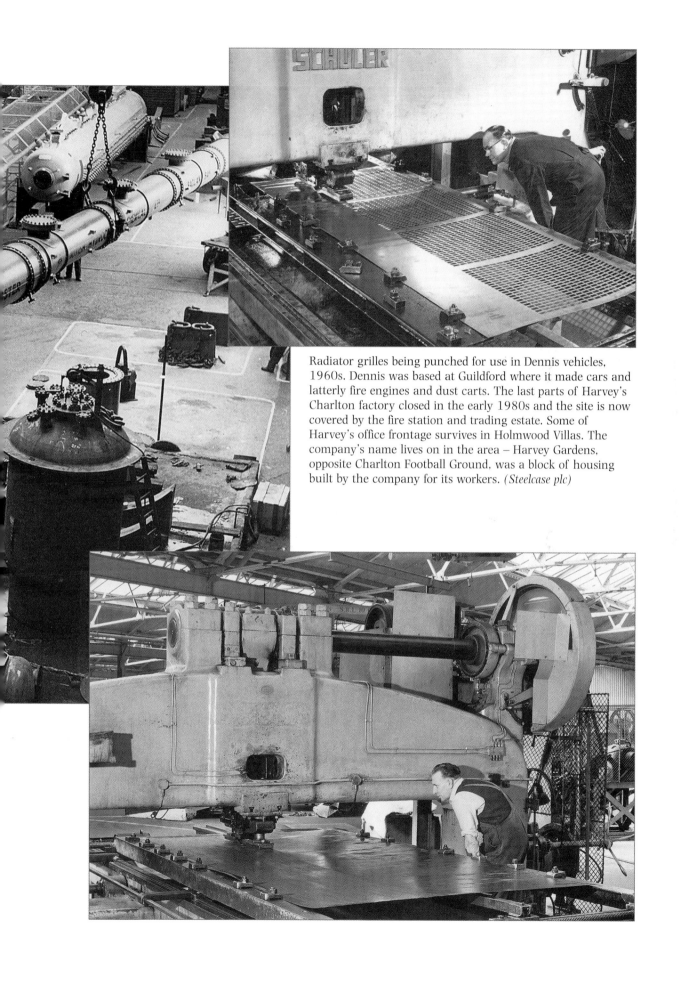

Radiator grilles being punched for use in Dennis vehicles, 1960s. Dennis was based at Guildford where it made cars and latterly fire engines and dust carts. The last parts of Harvey's Charlton factory closed in the early 1980s and the site is now covered by the fire station and trading estate. Some of Harvey's office frontage survives in Holmwood Villas. The company's name lives on in the area – Harvey Gardens, opposite Charlton Football Ground, was a block of housing built by the company for its workers. (*Steelcase plc*)

The Redpath Brown/Dorman Long works at Riverway on the Greenwich Peninsula became British Steel but was always known locally as 'Redpath's'. It was the sort of factory where several generations of the same family would work together. The company provided the structural steelwork for numerous buildings in London and the south-east, including the Royal Festival Hall. In this picture, taken in 1962, a special prototype lightweight riveting machine is being tested. *(Mr Fry, and thanks to Andrew Turner)*

A multi-spindle drilling plant being tested at the east Greenwich steelworks of Redpath Brown, 1962. It is designed for horizontal drilling. Redpath Brown was a Scottish company which opened its London site just before the First World War. After the factory closed some of the old sheds were converted into a trading estate by the Greater London Council. These were the last buildings to be demolished on the Millennium Dome site – a mere three weeks before the Experience opened. The factory canteen had been taken over by the Greenwich Yacht Club and that too was not demolished until the very last minute. Trespassing industrial archaeologists frantically tried to photograph and record the interiors of these buildings as they were stripped out on murky December days. *(Mr Fry, and thanks to Andrew Turner)*

Greenwich is world famous for the Royal Observatory and the work of the Astronomer Royal. Here an astronomer is seen in the Royal Observatory with his telescope. Greenwich was also a major centre for the manufacture of precision instruments. *(London Borough of Greenwich)*

W.H. Stanley was world famous for its scientific instruments. An enormous range was made at its factory in New Eltham. This picture shows the machine shop in the early 1950s. Other areas of the factory included a glass-blowers' department, a case and cabinet department, and an optical glass shop. Instruments were often produced with their own boxes, sometimes quite elaborately done with ivory inlays. A wide variety of speciality timbers were used in the factory. Stanley's closed in 2001. *(from Stanley Company History)*

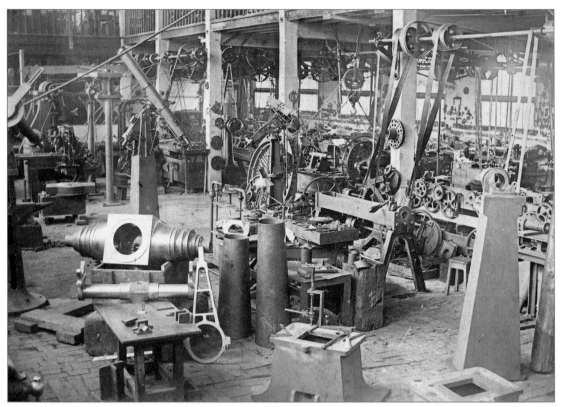

The machine shop at Troughton & Sims' Charlton works, 1880. The company began making mathematical instruments in 1688 and moved to Charlton in 1864. Its instruments were sent to observatories all over the world – Edward Troughton himself was a member of the Royal Astronomical Society and a bust of him is still owned by the Royal Observatory. The Altazimuth instrument, used to determine the exact position of a star in the sky, was developed at the works and accurate division was Troughton & Sims' speciality. It produced 'National Standard' measures for other nations, including Russia. *(London Borough of Greenwich)*

Collimation, a highly skilled task at Stanley's New Eltham instrument factory. Collimation is the process of adjusting parallel beams of light and is being used here to set up a sextant. *(from Stanley Company History)*

8

Diverse Trades

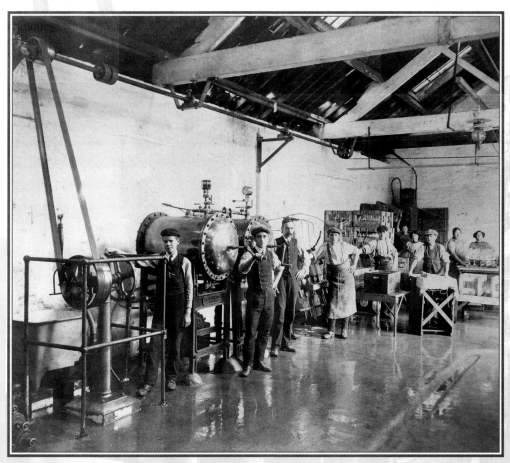

Willson's Horehound Brewery in Eastney Street, 1910. The workers are preparing a type of herb drink still sold in some parts of the world, particularly Australia where early settlers used it as a laxative and a sedative. It is a slightly fizzy brew made from hops and horehound, a medicinal plant with a bitter, robust flavour. The herbs are steeped in water and then boiled with sugar. The mixture is then fermented for twenty-four hours. Greenwich, Woolwich, Charlton, Plumstead and Eltham were home to an astonishing range of factories, workshops and other workplaces. Space allows only a few to appear in the following pages. The people employed in them came from a wide area of south London and Kent.
(London Borough of Greenwich)

Sand pits at Charlton, *c*. 1900. This area was known for the extraction of glass-making sand and the pits remained in use until the 1930s. There is a non-locomotive railway running on several levels and standing alone on one of the upper levels is a tipping wagon. This area is now part of a park.

Greenwich and Woolwich are full of holes – areas which were once pits for the extraction of sand or chalk. 'The Valley', in which Charlton football ground stands, is probably the best known and was operated by Lewis Glenton for chalk extraction in the nineteenth century. There are, however, many more around Maze Hill Station, on both sides of Blackheath Hill and at the old Southern Railway signal works alongside the Blackwall Tunnel approach road. There were also considerable underground workings for chalk extraction, perhaps the most notable being the Blackheath cavern underneath the Point which has often been described in terms more sensational than the chalk mine which it was in reality. Speculation and rumour have had it variously identified as a prehistoric temple and outlaws' hideout, among other things. There were also considerable underground workings in Wickham Lane, Plumstead and, most recently, chalk mining in the area of Abbey Wood around the Co-operative Estate. These chalk workings continued into the twentieth century and were operated by the Royal Arsenal Co-operative Society. Some buildings from the Abbey Wood mine remain on the site of the Abbey Wood Caravan Park. *(London Borough of Greenwich)*

Opposte top: Sugar and its associated products have been a major industry in east London for several centuries. This 1970s photograph shows the wharf wall of what was once Woolwich Dockyard but was later used by the Albion Sugar Co. A grain suction pipe is unloading sugar from a barge. Some of the flood defence work undertaken down river of the Thames Barrier is also visible. *(London Borough of Greenwich)*

Opposite bottom: Inside the works of Tunnel Glucose, *c*. 1960. Here glucose, a by-product of maize, is being dewatered. This is the refinery press floor and these are mud cake presses – filter presses used to remove the water from maize gluten 'mud' which was then dropped through the floor into skips below. Tunnel Glucose works still stands in Tunnel Avenue and is now owned by Amylum, part of Tate & Lyle. *(Tate & Lyle, and thanks to Ian Turner, Amylum plc)*

A lathe operator at the United Glass Works in Charlton, 1960s. This works was the largest bottle-making factory in Europe and the worker is turning steel moulds for the bottles, a job requiring a very high degree of skill. Glass-making had been established in the area since at least Tudor times because of the proximity to deposits of suitable sand. This bottle-making concern came to Charlton from north-east England and the huge factory was built in 1920. Even before the Second World War 200 million bottles were produced every year and this number increased significantly due to demand for medicine bottles following the foundation of the National Health Service. *(United Glass)*

A bottle is examined at the United Glass factory, Charlton, 1960s. These photographs are taken from publicity material aimed at the USA which stressed the high level of skills among south London workers. Despite this marketing effort the bottle works closed in 1966, partly because of the high wages needed to keep staff in south London. *(United Glass)*

Women war workers at the Kings Norton ammunition works, a private munitions factory on the Plumstead marshes. The factory was housed in huts north of the railway and west of Harrow Manor Way. The badges worn by the workers indicate that they are engaged in war work. The company was set up in 1890 at Kings Norton, near Birmingham, where it had a rolling mill but the loading plant was at Abbey Wood. The central figure may be John Shelley who was manager during the First World War.

A number of pictures appear in this book of women workers in wartime, some undertaking extremely dangerous and hazardous tasks. Many of them were employed in the explosives industries in 'danger' buildings. The work of women during the First World War in the Royal Arsenal is well known; they were sometimes called 'canaries' because exposure to the explosives – Lyddite or trinitriphenol – turned their skin yellow. Women had, however, been employed in explosives factories long before and in peacetime they were also employed in small firework factories, often privately run and extremely dangerous. A firework and flares factory on the Greenwich marshes employed women and girls who clearly came from the very poorest sections of society. This was skilled and difficult work and women were thought to be quicker, neater and probably safer at it. They were cheaper too. At the Kings Norton Works women filled explosive shells. The result of one of the explosions at this Greenwich factory is shown on page 100. *(London Borough of Greenwich)*

Employees at the Workshops for the Blind prepare a fendoff. The main workshops were at 166 Greenwich High Road and were founded in 1877 by the Naysmith Bequest. However, large items like this fendoff were made in what is now Feathers Place, Eastney Street. A local woman remembers going to visit her father who was one of the workers there. She found him 'in an open ended, cold, draughty building sitting on an iron bollard in the dark – the authorities must have thought the lights were wasted on blind men'. Fendoffs like this were common items on board vessels of all sizes and would have found a ready market in the surrounding river trades. (*London Borough of Greenwich*)

Making baskets at the Workshops for the Blind, Greenwich High Road. The business closed in the 1970s when the number of blind people interested in working there began to dwindle. The workshop site is now under the Ibis Hotel in Stockwell Street but some of the stonework has been used in the car park to the rear. The foreman at the Greenwich part of the workshop was known as Jim; he was sighted and was known locally as an accomplished singer. When the workshop closed he opened a small basketware shop in Greenwich High Road. (*London Borough of Greenwich*)

A Lennard tar still at the South Metropolitation Gas Company's Ordnance Wharf, *c.* 1890s. There had already been many years' tar processing at Ordnance Wharf before the gas company bought the site in the early 1880s. South Met seems to have inherited Mr Lennard and his continuous tar distillation system from earlier works on the site and nearby. Until 1957 there were two Lennard Continuous Stills at work together with a number of pot stills. *(Faye Gould)*

David Webb and William Pitts adjust the tar burners on a Lennard still's furnace, July 1952. Because the Lennard still was developed in Greenwich the workers at Ordnance Wharf became early experts in its operation. In due course some of them were to act world wide as advisors to future users of this sort of tar still. These pieces of equipment were important because the ideas behind them were taken over by the oil industry as a basis for the distillation of crude oil. *(Faye Gould)*

Sculpting the Great Globe (now at Durlston, Swanage) at Mowlem's Yard on the Greenwich Peninsula, 1887. Mowlem's had taken an early lease on one of the wharves built by Coles Child on the Greenwich riverside. The company later became Wimpey, and then Tarmac, which remained on the site until its lease expired in 2001. Mowlem had contracts for much of London's street maintenance and Swanage is littered with pieces of London's rejected stone work taken there by George Burt and his son George Mowlem Burt. The globe is 10 feet in diameter, weighs 40 tons and is made up of 15 segments of Portland Stone, which was quarried close to Swanage, taken to Greenwich, carved and then taken back! It is held together by granite dowels and is surrounded by seats and miscellaneous quotations. Cadet Place runs alongside the site on which the globe was carved and in the wall on the site there is an astonishing collection of miscellaneous stone off-cuts – perhaps some pieces of the globe are there too. *(Durlston Country Park)*

Listers made laundry machinery in Nightingale Vale, Woolwich. This photograph shows a specialist drying unit for chamois leathers. It was found in a derelict laundry building in the area and is assumed to show work at the factory. Natural light from windows illuminates the workbenches, the drying unit is in the centre and piles of finished materials are to the right. *(London Borough of Greenwich)*

A little-known trade in Woolwich was the manufacture of sports equipment, a real contrast to the big guns more usually associated with the town. These workers are with Grandidge, based in Plumstead. Founded in 1894 the company originally specialised in cricket bats – the 'Imperial Driver' was one of its lines. Grandidge advertised its interest in supplying to 'our foreign possessions' and also provided balls to Eton College. *(London Borough of Greenwich)*

Clarence print works. The legs of the supporting scaffolding are painted white, implying that this photograph was taken during wartime black-out, but the picture appears to be a lot older and remains something of a mystery. This is part of the Joseph Kaye development – now the Greenwich one-way system – and the scaffold implies some serious subsidence. Indeed, some cracking can be seen on the first-floor frontage of Mr Underwood's establishment. Next door is the Clarence Steam Printing Works, advertising itself as a 'bookbinders' with the ability to produce lithographs. No doubt it is the company's vans that are parked outside. *(London Borough of Greenwich)*

These two Victorian
craftsmen have prepared a
fine 'Invicta' for Blackheath
Drill Hall. It can be seen in
place in a drawing of the
opening ceremony in 1862.
The Drill Hall was in
Vanburgh Park, Blackheath,
and was used by the 3rd
West Kent Volunteers but
was burned down in the
early 1950s. The site is now
the Parkside flats. This
picture is perhaps a reminder
that Greenwich and
Woolwich – and of course
Blackheath – were very
much part of Kent until the
1880s. *(London Borough of
Greenwich)*

Motorcycles were one of Plumstead's best known products in the twentieth century. This is a dealer for the local
motorcycle company, Matchless. Behind the shop are the chimneys of Woolwich power station. AJS Motorcycles was
on the corner of Maxey Road and Burrage Grove. Matchless Motorcycles were made from 1899 but the factory closed
in 1969 after being taken over by Norton. *(London Borough of Greenwich)*

The blacksmiths' shop at Tilbury Contracting & Dredging Co.'s maintenance works, Providence Wharf, 1920s. Workshops like this were expected to turn out anything needed, to order and quickly. Skills had to be adaptable – and there was also a great need for lots of useful bits and pieces, so nothing was ever thrown away. *(London Borough of Greenwich)*

This drawing shows one of the two explosions at Robson & Dyer's ammunition works in the 1880s. The works was off Woolwich Road in Greenwich, roughly the site of the Caletock Estate, and made small-scale explosive items including caps, flares and specialist fireworks. In the first explosion two young women workers were killed (one on her first day at work) and two more died in the second. The picture shows one of the small, specially built, 'danger' buildings. Even today factories making this sort of item are required to build small units for one or two workers only, something that undoubtedly saved lives in this accident. Note the plot of cabbages growing around the damaged hut. The accident was investigated by Government Inspector Vivien Majendie whose home was nearby in Victoria Way and whose laboratory was at Woolwich in the Arsenal complex. *(London Borough of Greenwich)*

This crowd has come to see the aftermath of an accident. At 3.30 a.m. on 11 February 1907 the magazine of the Chemical Research Department in the Royal Arsenal blew to pieces and the gasholder of the Arsenal Gas Works then exploded. The explosion was heard 40 miles away and 30,000 window panes were broken. This picture shows shattered shopfronts and broken windows. *(London Borough of Greenwich)*

9

The Workforce in a Changing World

Sidney Frank Dean leaning on a lathe, October 1874. No more is known of this picture than Mr Dean's name so it is a matter of conjecture where the factory and the machine are. The best guess is that this is Penn's Marine Engine Works in Blackheath but it could be one of dozens of workplaces in Greenwich and Woolwich. *(London Borough of Greenwich)*

A group of children brought to Plumstead Library, given a book between every two of them, and no doubt told to keep still. The blurred heads show how bad they were at staying in one place! Woolwich Borough Council provided a library at Plumstead in 1904. It was opened in December of that year and was partly funded by the American steel magnate Andrew Carnegie. In the photograph it is a bare, spartan building with no books on shelves at all – a big contrast to today. (*London Borough of Greenwich*)

This is Quintin Hogg – not a Greenwich or Woolwich resident but important in that he was responsible for the movement which allowed for the foundation of Woolwich Polytechnic in the early 1890s. The polytechnic very much grew out of local efforts encouraged by Hogg and the ideas he had formulated at the Regent Street Polytechnic. Soon the Woolwich institution was able to provide a technical education for local young people. *(University of Greenwich)*

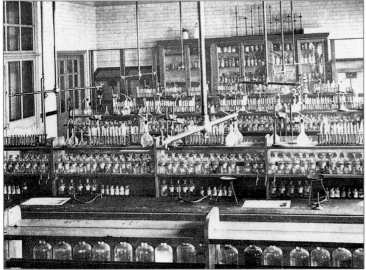

A skilled workforce needs to be well educated. Woolwich Polytechnic was the second in Britain and placed a strong emphasis on scientific education. This is the chemistry laboratory in 1892, one of several that provided an academic training to apprentices who were often on day release from work. There is a generation still alive who were apprentices at the Arsenal and trained here. They remember the old gas engine which was part of the apparatus in the old engineering laboratory. *(University of Greenwich)*

One of the least known institutions in the area was the Fuel Research Station at East Greenwich. It began life in 1917 as a government project to conduct studies of poison gases and was originally based inside the South Metropolitan Gas Works, the subjects being a personal interest of the Chairman, Dr Charles Carpenter. The station produced important research during the fifty or so years of its existence. For instance, during the Second World War its staff developed smoke-screening techniques. This picture shows the Chief Chemist at work. *(London Borough of Greenwich)*

Work under way at the Fuel Research Station. Greenwich Borough Museum acquired several boxes of these photographs, but they are not captioned and are often of apparatus which is experimental and probably, in its day, secret. It is therefore very difficult to know what they show. However, this one seems to involve some sort of test on different types of domestic grate. It also shows that women were employed along with men. *(London Borough of Greenwich)*

Siemens Brothers (latterly AEI) in the Woolwich Road maintained active and important research laboratories. This is the high voltage laboratory in 1960. A special building was erected to house this equipment with features to resist fire, mask out interference and take the weight of the equipment. Siemens' workforce was proud of the company's ability to stay in the forefront of telecommunications technology – and it was the firm's research arm that made this possible. (*John Ford and Siemens Engineering Society*)

Siemens' acoustic laboratory, all important in a factory where the main output was telephone equipment. The department's task was to maximise audio quality. Work was also carried out on behalf of other organisations. The picture dates from the late 1950s when the company was developing the 'Centenary Neophone', the first telephone to use printed circuit technology. (*John Ford and Siemens Engineering Society*)

A busy industrial area also produces a lot of unwanted and waste materials. This is Robinson's scrapyard at Anchor Iron Wharf in the 1960s; the company had been there since the 1830s. The wharf had been part of an early eighteenth-century anchor warehouse owned by Ambrose Crowley. The two workers are standing at the top of a set of traditional waterman's stairs – Golden Anchor Stairs. The wharf is a 'made up' one, that is it has been built out into the river beyond the original riverbank. In the nineteenth century scrap iron was transferred by hand-winch and wicker baskets but in later years more modern methods were used to handle the material which was sent to steelworks in Spain or Scotland for reprocessing. Behind the wharf are parts of Greenwich (London Transport) power station. Anchor Iron Wharf ceased to be used for scrap in the 1990s although Robinson's building remained with a commemorative plaque on the wall. Soon the site will be cleared to be replaced by public open space. *(Patricia O'Driscoll)*

Maybank's waste paper depot, 1970s. Jim Maybank described himself as the 'greatest totter in the business' and in the 1970s had premises in Charlton employing 500 people in the processing of waste paper. Maybank himself had come up through the rag-and-bone trade and realised the potential of waste paper during the war. He became the biggest dealer in Britain. *(London Borough of Greenwich)*

One of the biggest industries along the Greenwich riverside in the late twentieth century was the processing of building material, much of it used for great building projects in Docklands and other parts of London. Here stone chippings are stored in a pit, neatly surrounded by chain and bollards. This picture was taken on a site in Thames Street that borders Deptford Creek and was the location of a gas works that closed fifty or more years ago. This seems to be the remains of an old gasholder. Gasholders are like icebergs: they look big and impressive above ground but there is also an awful lot you cannot see underneath. The tank in which the iron bell would have fitted now seems to provide a handy storage area. *(Mary Mills)*

Roads and transport links need to be built and maintained if people and goods are to be moved about efficiently. Here a crowd has gathered to watch the laying of tarred blocks for tram lines in Nelson Road, Greenwich. The electric tram service began in 1904 so this photograph is likely to have been taken a year or so earlier. These tarred road blocks were made at a factory on the Greenwich Peninsula and used extensively in the late nineteenth and early twentieth centuries – they can still be found when roads are dug up, lying under the asphalt surface. Among the viewers, along with the usual small boys, is an unusually smart gent and a young woman, who may be with him. *(London Borough of Greenwich)*

Houses being demolished in King William Walk to make way for the extension of the Greenwich Railway, early 1870s. This break in the buildings is still only covered with lightweight constructions, although the Kings Arms pub in the foreground is still there but has been rebuilt. Health and safety are obviously not concerns here, even though the scene is clearly posed for the camera. *(London Borough of Greenwich)*

A fine steam crane and other equipment used for laying the Crossness storm water barrel drain between Plumstead and the Crossness Sewage Works, 1903. A note on the back of the picture says that the crane driver is Alf Waller, more usually known as 'Big Alf'. The storm water drainage system is important to south London since some areas are below high-tide level and the London County Council provided an extensive network to prevent flooding when drains could not cope with heavy rainfall. *(London Borough of Greenwich)*

Laying a gas main is a major piece of work requiring great planning. Here a gang from the South Metropolitan Gas Company lays a new length of main in Greenwich High Road in about 1900. *(from Co-partnership Journal)*

The construction of the Thames Barrier was a dramatic achievement for the Greater London Council. Completed in 1983, it is still a tourist attraction – and, of course, its real and most important role is to keep London safe from flooding. Greenwich and Woolwich people lived with the noise of the building work for years but as the project progressed the site became something of an attraction. Here one of the sections is being lifted into place by enormous cranes; this process took a long time and the huge section was lowered into place very slowly as it hung dramatically over the river. (*Howard Chard*)

On 27 October 1997 the trailing suction sand dredger *Sand Kite* hit the Thames Barrier on her way up river. She was loaded with 3,300 tons of sand and gravel and was trying to navigate in thick fog – an enquiry found that there was no effective lookout in place. Here *Sand Kite* is being removed by the tug *Sun Anglia*. The jumble of ships, cranes and barrier is very difficult to interpret and those of us who actually saw the operation were equally confused. It was a difficult and dangerous task to manoeuvre a substantial vessel off the barrier safely. However, this was later described as a 'textbook operation'. (*Alan Rose*)

The leisured Victorians – but this photograph is not entirely what it seems. It shows the Davies family in their beautiful garden next to their summerhouse. Mr Davies was the manager of a chemical works in Greenwich and the photograph was taken at the end of Riverway on the Peninsula. Riverway has now gone under the works for the Dome. Although everything looks peaceful, this picture was taken literally yards away from the huge chemical plant and not very far from the newly built East Greenwich Gas Works. Cory's *Atlas* coal transfer system is moored out in the river (see page 19). These people are standing in a noisy, dirty, polluted place, something with which Greenwich inhabitants were only too familiar. *(Major Wagstaff)*

Buster Bloodvessel and Desmond Dekker at the Mitre. This pub provided beer for thirsty gas workers at the East Greenwich Gas Works. In the 1980s it found a new role as the Tunnel Club, pioneering stand-up comedy and 'pub rock'. Several of those who survived the lively and critical audiences at the club went on to become major stars, among them Julian Clary and Jennie Eclair. The Tunnel Club itself moved to a location in central Greenwich under the redoubtable Malcolm Hardee and still provides an entertaining night out. *(Mary Mills)*

The contrast of old and new – the Royal Yacht *Britannia* passing Greenwich on her farewell visit to the capital, 2001. Unusually, and quite like old times, the river is full of ships. Some are just passing on the tide but many more have come to see the old yacht. A fire float is in the foreground with all its pumps throwing water in the air in time-honoured fashion. Straight ahead is the modern world embodied by the single tower of Canary Wharf. To the right of it, behind the ship, are the masts of the Dome and alongside it the vent for the Blackwall Tunnel. *(Howard Chard)*

A jobs fair for young people, early 1970s. This school leaver has come to see what is on offer from a whole variety of different employers. What she chooses is likely to be very different from what was on offer to young women fifty years ago. Jobs in industry have gone, both those in heavy trades and on assembly work. She is sitting at an electric typewriter but that too would soon be obsolete and, having learnt how to use it, she would be obliged to start again to acquire computer skills if she were to remain employable. *(London Borough of Greenwich)*

A woman arc welder at Johnson & Phillips cable factory. In both world wars women took on the hard and heavy jobs usually only performed by men. When the wars were over the men returned to the assembly lines. *(Delta plc)*

Nichol's pottery at Charlton, 1970s. The pottery stood in the Woolwich Road and in its latter days mainly produced elements for gas fires. Its raw materials came from a pit near Coulsden in Surrey although at one time local material was used; in fact, local raw materials were the reason Nichol's moved to Greenwich in the first place. The kiln – with its distinctive 'N' for Nichol – was in the back and proximity to terraced housing can be seen in the picture. At the front was a rather grand-looking house, itself standing in a terrace. *(London Borough of Greenwich)*

By the time the pottery closed in the 1970s local historians were becoming conscious of the need to make a record of local industry, which was beginning to wind down in Greenwich and Woolwich. Here an archaeologist is entering the now deserted pottery to take photographs and try to record the remains. *(London Borough of Greenwich)*

Industrial remains have been preserved in Greenwich for a long time. This picture dates from the early 1900s and shows the gateway to the East Greenwich Gas Works Ordnance Wharf chemical works. Piled up by the gate are half-made guns left by the Blakely Ordnance Wharf which stood here in the nineteenth century. Blakely had gone bankrupt when the works, and the guns, were only half finished and the site had been deserted. No doubt the gas company found the large pieces of metal difficult to dispose of and thought they might make an attractive decorative feature. These guns would now be valuable collector's pieces sought after by museums but British Gas sold them for scrap in the 1970s. *(from Co-partnership Journal)*

A more modern memorial to past industry: in 2001 this mural by the Greenwich Mural Workshop was installed in what appears to be a pedestrian underpass in Woolwich but was in fact a railway tunnel into Woolwich Dockyard. The mural celebrates the history of Woolwich Dockyard – to the left a great ship is launched and in the centre is the Clock House building. The mural was prepared and designed by the workshop in collaboration with local young people who wanted to learn the special mosaic technique used to make it. It is hoped the mosaic will be resistant to all-pervasive graffiti. *(Greenwich Co-operative Development Agency)*

Greenwich is now regarded as a tourist area. Visitors have come to the Borough since the eighteenth century to see the river, the hospital and the park, but this process has accelerated since the Second World War. This is Cutty Sark Gardens in the 1950s when the area was being prepared for the arrival of the famous sailing clipper. Since then the ship has become a well-known symbol of the area, despite the fact that it was built on the Clyde. Although the shops still stand, small streets used by fishermen and other river trades were demolished to bring the ship in. Part of Greenwich pier was also demolished to allow the ship into her dry dock, and then rebuilt once she was safely there. *(London Borough of Greenwich)*

A view the tourists never see: repair work on the roof of the Neptune Hall at the National Maritime Museum, 2001. From this unusual position the Royal Observatory and planetarium can be seen on the hill above. The National Maritime Museum has expanded dramatically to meet the expectations of the hordes of visitors but constant maintenance is needed to keep abreast of demand. *(Chris Stevens/London Borough of Greenwich)*

Councillors and officers from the London Borough of Greenwich walk along Ballast Quay in the late 1970s. Led by Councillor Derek Penfold, the party includes Chris Field, Director of Leisure Services, Julian Watson, Local History Librarian, and Councillor Phil Graham – and hidden behind them somewhere are Local History Librarian Barbara Ludlow and Councillor Jim Gillman. They walked along the pathway between the *Cutty Sark* and Morden Wharf in the hope of discovering the tourist potential of the industrial riverside as factories and wharves began to close. *(London Borough of Greenwich)*

A band of enthusiastic environmentalists and ecologists examine the Deptford Creek's bed, 2001. Above them towers the Aston Webb-designed Mumford's flour mill. Out of use as a mill for many years, it is now listed and about to be converted into flats. Deptford Creek is actually the mouth of the River Ravensbourne and this hitherto neglected industrial waterway has become a feature of the area which can be exploited for tourists with an interest in the natural world, although there has been very little natural here for some centuries. In the late 1990s Greenwich Community College began to run courses for students who want to learn how to make a living from 'eco-tourism'. *(London Borough of Greenwich)*

Young men on a training scheme
manhandle an iron cover from a tomb
in Woolwich church yard, 1979. The
tomb is that of the innovative
Woolwich-born engineer Henry
Maudslay. It had been discovered that
renovation work in the churchyard was
endangering the commemorative
plaque and a local group of enthusiasts
had managed to recruit these young
men to help save it. *(Jack Vaughan
collection)*

The group displays the iron plate commemorating the life of Henry Maudslay. In the back row are three
enthusiasts who managed to get the job done – left to right: Alan Pearsall, Ralph Burnett and Jack
Vaughan. They felt very strongly that the area was ignoring its industrial heritage and in particular the
contribution that Woolwich engineers had made to the wider world of invention and enterprise. Part of
the incentive for recovering this plate was to make the point that we should keep alive some memories of
past achievements. The plate was taken to the Borough Museum and it is hoped it will be displayed in
the new Heritage Centre at Woolwich Arsenal. *(Jack Vaughan collection)*

Cubow's Yard at Woolwich, 1980s. Boat-building and repair on the Thames are still emotive subjects for many people and it is proving hard to let it go. The reopening of this yard caused some local excitement, but the work was short-lived and the site now stands derelict awaiting building work to start on up-market flats and a hotel. On the river the Woolwich Ferry can be seen taking local children for a day out. *(London Borough of Greenwich)*

'Kenny's Jetty', 1998. As one industry moves away so others move in. This is the old Redpath Brown Jetty on the Greenwich Peninsula which was taken over by an unofficial breakaway yacht club. The club, under the leadership of Kenny Hillbrown, remained enthusiastically active for some years, but was considered too scruffy to be in the vicinity of the Millennium Dome. Despite a lively campaign in the press Kenny and his jetty were swept away and no sign of them remains. *(Mary Mills)*

An isolated reminder of the Borough's rural past, 1908. This tithe barn was at Manor Farm, Plumstead, in an area north-east of the parish church and now covered by Benares Road. The barn survived, despite housing development, until 1908. In this picture, taken just before demolition, the old thatched and dilapidated structure is still being used as a store by W.J. Hart, building contractor. (*London Borough of Greenwich*)

'A RURAL SCENE AT EAST GREENWICH.' Is this picture a joke? It appears with no explanation in the South Metropolitan Gas Company's house magazine for 1910. It shows Tunnel Avenue, Greenwich, with No. 1 gasholder behind and the trees along the road are still little more than saplings. Today Tunnel Avenue is lined with houses but the gasholder and trees are still there. What is this haystack? A great deal of land in this area was used for allotments by gas company employees and others. Did they build it? Or was it in fact for hay to feed horses belonging to Wheatley's cab company and probably still grazed in some of the adjoining fields? *(from Co-partnership Journal)*

Mr W. Cook of Cook's Farm Wickham Lane ploughs his remaining fields as the houses encroach ever nearer, 1920s. Some farming remained on the outskirts of Greenwich and Woolwich as late as the 1980s and still persists on the Eltham borders. Wickham Lane is at the far eastern edge of the Borough and open land in that area was taken for housing in the 1930s and 1950s. *(London Borough of Greenwich)*

Some farming still remained in the Borough into the 1980s. Woodlands Farm on Shooters Hill was owned by the Royal Arsenal Co-operative Society and here a combine harvester is at work in the fields. The farm's north-eastern border is very near to Wickham Lane and Cook's Farm, which appears in the picture at the top of the page. These fields were used to grow barley in the 1970s and '80s. It was used to feed pigs raised on the farm and the animals at the abattoir, which was hidden in the woods at the top end of the farm. *(RACS archive)*

Woodlands Farm, 2001. The old Royal Arsenal Co-operative Society farm on Shooters Hill is now a charitable trust keeping sheep, cattle and other livestock. The slaughterhouse has been pulled down and the site is used as a dump for the Borough's recycled green waste scheme. *(Ian Boulton, Woodlands Farm Trust)*

Thomas and Merlin at Woodlands Farm, 2001. The two horses on Shooters Hill are proving a big attraction with visitors and passers by but also work hard for their living. Woodlands is not an 'urban city farm' but a real farm, with proper fields – and proper working horses. *(Ian Boulton, Woodlands Farm Trust)*

Snowy wastes and a derelict gas works site: this picture was taken in 1986 when the works had largely been demolished and open space had suddenly appeared. In the following years, and before the land was cleared for the Dome, a sizeable wood grew up in this area. In some places pools began to appear where pools and ditches had existed before the gas works was built in the 1880s. Although the gas works followed the pattern of earlier fields, the designers of the Dome did not do this and an artificial landscape has now been imposed. In the foreground is rubble and the remains of the East Greenwich gas works. Some of the blocks come from the demolition of the No. 2 gasholder. *(Mary Mills)*

At one time a railway went into the gas works on the Peninsula, taking goods traffic which had come down the 'Angerstein Line' and crossed a road called Riverway. This bridge was demolished in the 1980s, although the embankment for the line remained. When preparations for the Dome began the bridge was rebuilt and the old line used as a route for lorries entering the site. Eventually road, bridge and embankment were all demolished and today this site can only be traced with great difficulty. *(Mary Mills)*

10
Building the Dome

The erection of the Dome was an exciting event for local people and for those who pass the site
every day on their way through the Blackwall Tunnel. Day by day we watched and waited,
speculating on what was going on as the structure rose higher and higher. This is one of the
concrete anchor blocks for the Dome's masts under construction. Piles have been driven into
the mud of the Peninsula and this framework built on top.
(Chris Stevens/London Borough of Greenwich)

The first stage of the Dome's masts was built on top of concrete anchor blocks. Their height can be judged against the workers alongside. (*Chris Stevens/London Borough of Greenwich*)

The Dome begins to rise above Greenwich. This picture was taken from the railway bridge on Halstow Road. The masts of the Dome are in place and the central structure is beginning to rise up in a mass of scaffolding. All around are the relics of past – and present – industry. On the far left is the Greenwich No. 1 gasholder – once the largest in the world, an early 'modern' industrial structure, and reputedly much disliked by the Dome's designers. Next to it the vent of the 'new' Blackwall Tunnel will soon be incorporated into the structure of the Dome. In front of the gasholder are the old Dreadnought School and the traffic control gantry on the Blackwall Tunnel approach. In front of the Dome is the last shed of Hay's chemical warehouse and stretching to the right of it the vacant land on which the Millennium Village is now being built. The river is out of sight but many of the buildings to be seen are on the other side of it: right of the gasholder is the Reuters building on the site of the Blackwall Yard ship repair works and Mulberry Place, currently Tower Hamlets Town Hall, on the site of the East India Dock. To the right of the Dome are the gasholders at Leven's Road holder station in Poplar. (*Howard Chard*)

The mast is finally in place and workers are hoisted to the top in a cradle. There are twelve of these masts and they were lifted in just two weeks. Once they were fixed work on the central section and the roof could begin. *(Chris Stevens/London Borough of Greenwich)*

Workers on the roof of the Dome – roped as if they were mountain climbing – 'stitch' the sections together by hand. These workers were specialists in abseiling but the wind that whips round the Peninsula at all times made their work even more difficult and dangerous. *(Chris Stevens/ London Borough of Greenwich)*

The vent of the Blackwall Tunnel as the roof of the Dome is built around it. This is the vent for the 'new' tunnel built in the 1960s. The taller column is the vent and the shorter is the fresh air intake. A special hole was provided in the roof of the Dome to allow the column to continue in its role of venting the tunnel. *(Chris Stevens/London Borough of Greenwich)*

Legs protrude into the exhibition area. A local woman, Barbara Barwick, who worked in the Dome, commented: 'This is "Body Explore" – so much more interesting and "hands on" than the Body itself. If only people had given up queuing for the Body and spent more time on these interactive exhibits, they'd have had more fun.' Most of the Greenwich people who worked in the Dome during millennium year regarded it as a training experience and went off to other jobs. (*English Partnerships*)

'Elvis on Stilts'. The Millennium Experience was fun for visitors but hard work for the huge team who provided entertainment for them every day. This group is one of many who mingled with the crowds. Elvis on Stilts have the letters E, L, V and I on their backs – no S. So depending how they stand they spell 'LIVE', 'EVIL' or just plain 'VILE'. Inside the central arena a team of specially trained acrobats and trapeze artists provided one of the most spectacular features, filling the space from floor to roof with smoke and noise described as 'totally brilliant – by far the best part of the Experience and definitely not to be missed'. (*Keith Ward*)

ACKNOWLEDGEMENTS

Julian Watson, Francis Ward and staff at Woodlands Local History Library; Beverley Burford and Chris Ford at Greenwich Borough Museum; Len Riley and Southwark Local History Library; Jack Vaughan; Forbo Nairn; Kim Elms of Cory Environmental; Reg Barter; Peter Guillery; Delta plc; Ron Roffey and RACS Archive; Shaw Lovell; John Ford and the Siemens Engineering Society; Howard Chard; Jim Lee; Isobel Lilley and the Independent Photography Project; Archivist at the City of Saskatoon; Malcolm Tucker; John Day and the Ordnance Society; Tim Smith; R.J.M. Carr; Pam Carr; Andrew Turner; Mr & Mrs Fry; Ian Turner and Amylum plc; Barbara Ludlow; United Glass; Faye Gould; Durlston Country Park; Paul Stigant and the Archivist University of Greenwich; Alan Rose; Maj Wagstaff; Keith Ward; Ian Boulton and Woodlands Farm Trust; Steelcase plc; Chris Stevens and Greenwich Building Surveyors; Catherine Snow and English Partnerships – and most of all Alan Mills.